Unconditional

Bliss

Unconditional

Bliss

Finding Happiness in the Face of Hardship

• • •

An Introduction to LIVING THE QUESTIONS *by*

Howard Raphael Cushnir

A publication supported by
THE KERN FOUNDATION

Quest Books
Theosophical Publishing House

Wheaton, Illinois ♦ Chennai (Madras), India

First Quest Edition 2000

The Theosophical Publishing House
P.O. Box 270
Wheaton, IL 60189-0270

A publication of the Theosophical Publishing House,
A department of the Theosophical Society in America

Cover and book design and typesetting by Beth Hansen-Winter

Library of Congress Cataloging-in-Publication Data
Cushnir, Howard.
Unconditional bliss: finding happiness in the face of hardship: an introduction to living the questions / by Howard Raphael Cushnir. — 1st Quest ed.

     p. cm.
"A publication supported by the Kern Foundation."
"Quest books."
ISBN 0-8356-0792-5
1. Conduct of life.   I. Kern Foundation.   II. Title.
BF637.C5 C87 2000
299'.936—dc21   00-034391

6   5   4   3   2   1   *   00   01   02   03   04   05

Printed in the United States of America

For Josh Baran and Mary Beth Albert

MY BEAUTIFUL BEACONS OF BLISS

Contents

Part Three – Advanced Bliss

Part Four – Beyond Bliss

". . . Be patient toward all that is unsolved

in your heart and try to love the questions themselves like locked

rooms and like books that are written in a very foreign tongue

. . . . The point is to live everything. Live the questions now."

—RAINER MARIA RILKE

Introduction

EVERYONE WANTS TO FEEL GOOD. NATU-rally, we gravitate toward activities which give us pleasure and avoid those which give us pain. For some, this involves all kinds of sophisticated strategy and delayed gratification. For others, it's as simple as going out and doing what they love.

All human beings are complicated, and each human being is unique. As a result, there are countless variations in the pursuit of pleasure. Often, our histories and life circumstances provide serious obstacles along the way. Even if those obstacles are surmounted, most of us possess deeply held beliefs about how much pleasure we're *allowed* to have.

What unites most people in their pursuit of pleasure is the idea that it arises as a response to experience. Sex, money, power, love — these are all seen as exceptional triggers. At the same time, thoughtful people understand that none of those triggers will succeed in providing lasting pleasure unless a person's inner environment can foster and sustain it.

In the pursuit of inner peace, we spend countless hours and billions of dollars. Our investments go to books, therapies, retreats, and techniques such as yoga and meditation. We hope that by becoming better, happier people, our actual experience of life will brighten as well.

This approach often leads to great success. We flow with life more easily and take things more in stride. But life is still hard, for everyone, and great suffering never fails to make an appearance at many points along the way. No amount of inner work, for example, can prepare us for the death of a loved one. In fact, most people would argue that it *shouldn't*. To be fully engaged in life, the argument goes, means taking whatever comes and responding to it deeply and authentically.

I agree with this argument, but it only tells half the story. I try to tell the other half in this book.

Imagine an existence of constant, ever-available bliss. Imagine that this bliss asks for nothing and depends on nothing. Imagine that it is the very foundation of all experience, and that not even the most tragic of life's events can alter its strength or presence.

I know that this bliss exists. I know it because I live it. And I believe that you can, too.

What's more, in order to live in the radiance of this bliss, you don't need to be like me or anyone else. You don't need to have faith in God or any creed. Whether you're shy or loud, Christian or atheist, revolutionary or archconservative, this bliss belongs to you.

"All right then," you must be asking, "so where is it?" The answer is simple. The bliss to which I'm referring is deep within every one of us, always present but rarely chosen. To choose it requires the asking of just two questions. We need to ask these questions with great patience and intention. We need to embody them, to live them.

In this brief text I attempt to describe the questions, explore them, and provide you with everything necessary to make them your own. If you stick it out to the end and begin living the questions, you may soon taste a bliss as eternal as it is indescribable.

The book begins with a quick orientation — *Terms of Service* — which explains how I came to write it and suggests a framework in which to approach it. *Part Two — Basic Bliss* provides a foundation for the questions, clarifies them, and then demonstrates how to put them to use. This first pass is elementary, and therefore avoids many subtleties and complications. *Part Three — Advanced Bliss* fills in those missing pieces. *Part Four — Beyond Bliss* explores how living the questions can radically transform our entire perspective.

How you read the book should be determined by what you bring to it. If you're intrigued by what you've read so far, then proceed from start to finish. If you're impatient, and want to get to the bliss right away, then skip immediately to chapter 4. If you're deeply resistant, perhaps not even sure it's worth continuing, then first visit chapter 17, which addresses the most prevalent dissenting views. If at any time along the way you despair, and suspect that the circumstances of your life preclude bliss, then quickly flip to chapter 25. There, we'll investigate some common roadblocks, as well as practical steps to work through them.

No matter how you arrive, I sincerely hope you make it through. If so, you won't need to learn about bliss the way I did, which costs a lot more and hurts a lot worse.

Finally, it needs to be said that nothing in this book belongs to me. The bliss, as well as the questions that lead to it, are a product of the great mystery at the source of all existence. I bow to that source, revel in it, and one day hope to meet you there.

PART ONE

• • •

Terms of Service

CHAPTER 1

How I Know about Bliss

FOR OVER TWENTY YEARS, WITH a seeker's heart and a skeptic's mind, I roamed widely in the spiritual marketplace. I explored my own heritage — Judaism — as well as any other traditions that sparked me. Throughout my investigations, I vowed not to accept anything on faith that I didn't experience directly. Except for a few peak experiences, I encountered no bliss whatsoever.

On the other hand I wasn't complaining. I considered myself a fortunate person. I was blessed with many advantages and had chalked up many achievements. I grew up in a difficult family (who doesn't?) but had worked hard to heal most of my wounds. My career and personal life were on track. I had my health. I anticipated life's ups and downs and managed them reasonably well.

And then, all of a sudden, everything exploded. The details of that tragedy aren't the subject of this book. What's important, though, is how deeply miserable I became. All my assumptions about life went right out the window. At the age of thirty-four, I felt like I knew absolutely nothing.

Eventually, that explosion came to serve me. I was cracked open, defenseless, and the hole left behind was wide enough for grace to enter. By grace, I don't mean anything religious at all. There was no "seeing the light" or accepting a savior or coming to a deeper understanding. In my case, grace meant the arrival of an inner transformation. Spontaneously, and without effort, my experience of living was suddenly and irrevocably changed.

In my core, in the region we call the heart, arose the ceaseless experience of bliss. For no reason whatsoever, I felt joyous and peaceful and loving. At first I thought it was a mood or another peak experience that would surely pass. But it hasn't, to this day, and that was a full five years ago.

So there I was, the same guy as before with the same rotten life, except instead of feeling rotten it felt spectacular. The bliss in my heart radiated throughout my body, and beyond, to anyone open to receive it.

On top of all that, nothing seemed to be required of me in order for the bliss to continue. It was a mysterious gift with no strings attached.

From the outset, I decided to pay very close attention to what was happening. I felt like my own life now contained the message I'd long been seeking, and I wasn't going to let that message elude me.

It didn't. I got it. And now I pass it along to you.

CHAPTER 2

Don't Believe a Word I Say

USUALLY, IN A BOOK LIKE THIS, the writer presents a thesis and then sets out to prove it. You, the reader, follow the writer's train of thought. In the end, if you make it that far, you decide whether to agree or disagree.

Often, you're swayed a bit by the position and reputation of the writer. You probably choose to read the book in the first place because you have reason to respect the writer's opinions. Maybe the writer is a renowned expert or can document years of study on the topic in question.

In this book, however, I don't attempt to prove anything. Nor do I claim even a shred of expertise. I don't expect you to trust what I say, and in fact I hope you won't.

Instead, I'll present you with a series of observations from my own life. These observations have led me to believe that the direct experience of bliss is available right now, and all the time, to virtually every human being.

Does that sound outrageous? It might to me, if I were in your place. But I hope, as you read further, that you'll come to know this for yourself.

That won't happen because my observations make sense. Even if they do, and you accept them as your own, nothing but your beliefs will change. And the goal here is something much more profound.

I invite you to doubt my observations like a reasonable and skeptical scientist. I invite you to put them to the test in your own life. I invite you to experience this bliss when it's easy, when it's a challenge, and when it seems utterly impossible. Only then, if it happens, will you share the gift that was given to me.

CHAPTER 3

This Is Not a New Age Book

THIS IS NOT A NEW AGE BOOK. In fact it's nearly the opposite. Perhaps you're wondering why this bears mention. The answer lies in what the New Age label represents.

In my experience, two key tenets are at the core of most New Age thought. The first is that each of us creates our own reality, from the world we see around us to the world we find within. According to this logic, anything we don't like we can change. The trick is to learn how we've made it so and then redirect that same process to manifest a new result.

Approaching life this way can lead to valuable self-empowerment. Many people employ it to uncover limiting personal beliefs. From my perspective, however, it can overemphasize the amount of control we actually have. It can lead us to blame ourselves, falsely, for the circumstances of our lives. Sometimes, in addition, it can allow us to deny what is. And denial of what is, as we'll soon discover, actually prevents change from taking place.

The second core New Age tenet is that each one of us possesses unlimited potential. If we can merely tap this potential, then all the love, health, success, power, and money in the world will be ours. Most of the books, tapes, and seminars of the New

Age movement offer techniques for unleashing that potential.

This book isn't one of them. Though health, success, power, and money are often a by-product of living the questions, they are never the goal. Our focus will remain on moment to moment experience, not results. In fact, what we'll be exploring here is a bliss that has nothing to do with the particulars of your life.

The claim I make is this: You can live in bliss even if you're alone, sick, failed, and broke. Not that I expect that, or wish it upon you, but it's certainly one hundred percent possible.

What we'll examine in the following pages is an outlook that separates our state of being from all we do or don't achieve. We're free to go about our business, but don't depend upon it for personal satisfaction.

Does that make any sense? Would you accept if it were true? Perhaps, like so many, you're attached to the idea that how you feel is the result of what happens in your life.

If so, for just a few hours, I invite you to suspend that assumption entirely.

PART TWO

• • •

Basic Bliss

CHAPTER 4

A Defining Moment

THINK OF AN ACTIVITY THAT gives you great joy. This could be singing, reading, hiking, or even watching your favorite TV show. Once you've selected the activity, pause for a few seconds and summon up the feeling that the activity generates.

Next, think of a person whom you love as much as anyone on earth. If no one springs quickly to mind, choose instead a pet or even a place. Once you've selected your love, pause for a few seconds and conjure up the feeling it elicits.

Now take a deep breath, smile, and bring that joy and love together. Let yourself sink into the experience this creates. Plain and simple, it's bliss.

Joy + Love = Bliss

That is the formula, only we need to add a refinement. As long as this bliss is centered on an action, or a thing, it's bound to come and go. This type of bliss is therefore temporary, and that's not what we're after. A more accurate formula would be:

Joy + Love - Cause = Permanent Bliss

If you feel like it, give yourself a taste of this right now. Call up your previous two "causes," let the bliss flow, and then consciously allow the causes to fall away. If you stay with the feeling, with the experience of bliss, it won't fall away as well. Not for awhile, at least, until your mind jumps on board a new tangent.

In my own life, I've come to see that bliss is present all the time. It's truly permanent. And this is a great relief, because it means that I don't have to create it. But while bliss is always there, I'm not always there with it. Sometimes I choose to go elsewhere, and other times I'm swept away by one of many habits and patterns.

Of course I'm not alone in this. Essentially, it's the human condition. The problem we all face in our lives is not how to create more bliss, or even how to find it, but simply how to guarantee access.

CHAPTER 5

Contracting and Expanding

THINK OF SOMEONE OR SOME-
thing that you really can't stand. Make sure this choice is one of
your worst sore spots, that it frustrates and angers you to no end.
Once you've got it, let yourself well up with these negative emotions. Go for it with gusto, until your whole being seems to brim
with agitation.

Now take a step back mentally and observe the result. Do a
quick scan of your physical sensations. Notice what it feels like
to be *in* your body during such an experience. Notice where in
your body all of those unpleasant feelings concentrate.

If you're like most people, this experience is one of clenching
and constricting. Your whole body goes into a state of contraction. The contraction begins in your gut but almost immediately
spreads outward, often concentrating in your shoulders and breath.

Being contracted is being closed. You're alive to the sensations in your body but dead to what's happening beyond it. Or, if
you're one of those people like me who use thinking to keep from
feeling, you might not even be alive to your body. Instead, you
might unconsciously be trying to think your way out of all that
tension.

Bliss, on the other hand, is all about being open. The more

you feel it, the more you expand. As opposed to the gut where contraction starts, expansion begins in the heart. It, too, spreads throughout the body, creating relaxation like a warm, inner bath.

Upon reading this, it might seem that contracting is bad and expanding is good. But that's not the point at all. Contracting and expanding are the way of life and particularly the way of human beings. Even when we don't encourage the process willfully, our bodies still contract and expand on their own. No matter how many advances we make in energy science and mind-body medicine, there will still be such a thing as waking up on the wrong side of the bed.

With regard to energy science and mind-body medicine, it's common in some circles to talk about esoteric concepts like opening and aligning the "chakras." In addition, we may sometimes hear about the "subtle body," the "mental body," and the "emotional body." In another context, these terms may be useful and important. Here, however, they're much too elusive and complex.

All you need to know about energy, as far as bliss is concerned, is this fundamental dance of contraction and expansion. When you're feeling clenched and agitated, that's contraction. When you're feeling joyous and loving, that's expansion. And when you're not feeling much of anything at all, then you're somewhere in between.

I encourage you to investigate this yourself. Give it a day or so. With a watch, an alarm, or merely a mental monitor, check your state of being about every fifteen minutes. Do a quick body scan and see where you fall on the scale. If you get lost in the flow of the day and can't report as you go, then look backward in the evening and recall your major highs and lows.

Expand and contract, expand and contract. It's as natural and automatic as breathing in and breathing out.

Our goal, remember, is to guarantee access to bliss. Understanding contraction and expansion is the first step. From there, we can see that access to bliss becomes available only with expansion.

But if bliss requires expansion, and it's a natural cycle for us to expand *and* contract, then how can we ever experience constant bliss?

The answer arises from paying a closer look at the causes of contraction. Forget about expansion. If we're fully there, and if we choose bliss, then the floodgates open and we're instantly suffused. But contraction is where all of us dam the works. And though a bit of that's inevitable, the vast majority we bring upon ourselves.

CHAPTER 6

Resistance

WHENEVER WE DON'T LIKE or don't want something, we automatically contract against it. It's an unconscious process, equally true about a nasty comment, a lover's betrayal, or a terminal illness. Because the process is so wide-ranging, it happens literally hundreds of times a day.

Think about it, or better yet imagine your way into it. Picture yourself getting cut off on the highway by a manic driver. What happens? You contract. Now imagine stubbing your toe. Your whole body goes taut from the pain. An overdrawn checking account, a critical parent, a mealy apple — they all lead to the same *physical* reaction.

At the same time, each situation may elicit a particular *emotional* response. We may be afraid, angry, or disgusted. Different emotions affect us in different ways. But the whole array of unpleasant feelings, despite its surface variation, arises from the same type of core contraction. And we can't help any of this, either. It's hardwired deep in our circuitry.

Every single one of these reactions is completely instantaneous. But when we hold onto the contraction after that instant is over, when we align ourselves with its rigid quality, that's a personal choice. We are choosing resistance. And what are we resisting? Something which already exists.

Resistance is a denial of what is, and as such, it's a wasted effort. What's worse, it keeps us from the expansion which allows for bliss.

Let's look at two brief examples. First, imagine you have a truly annoying new coworker. The worst thing about him is his screechy laugh. Every time he lets one out, you want to reach over and strangle him. You would never do it, but that's the initial reaction. You want this guy gone, for good.

So you sit at your desk, taut, just waiting for the guy to walk by. When he does, you tense up even further, and at lunchtime you commiserate with your associates. All afternoon it's hard to concentrate. You stew about it on the ride home. You try to think about something else, but it keeps popping back up. You tell yourself, "Let it go, let it go," since you know that's the "spiritual" thing to do, but obviously you're not spiritual because that doesn't work either.

This relatively minor nuisance, due to your resistance, has quickly become a pervasive poison.

Next, imagine you've been dating someone for awhile. You're falling in love. You want it to develop into a lasting relationship, but you're not sure if your lover's onboard. Every time you begin to raise the subject, you can't go through with it. You're paralyzed with fear. What if your affection isn't returned? It'll be too hurtful to bear.

Over time you grow nervous and awkward. You're even a little resentful that your lover hasn't brought the subject up for you.

When you finally can't wait any longer and try to speak your truth, all that pent-up anxiety makes you tongue-tied. You begin to whine, to blame, to self-destruct with insecurity and frustration. Your lover, not surprisingly, backs off. Was it you, or just your delivery? You'll never get to know.

In this case, things are a bit more subtle. You've resisted the *possibility* that your love might not be reciprocated. Something which hadn't even come to pass caused a prolonged contraction with the worst possible consequence.

Resistance occurs when we cling to contraction. Throughout the book, we'll look at many more examples. Hopefully, at least one of them will hit close to home. It's crucial for you to relate to this idea experientially, to recognize in yourself the ways you contract and then choose to stay there.

"But what else am I supposed to do?" you may protest. "When I'm annoyed or afraid, to pretend otherwise would just be faking." If you *are* having a reaction like this, it's a great opportunity to examine resistance. Right now, in real time, notice where it lingers in your body. Don't attempt to understand it, remove it, or change it. Instead, just see if you can meet it with acceptance.

CHAPTER 7

Acceptance

"THERE IS NOTHING UNWORTHY of acceptance." I remember distinctly the first time I heard that phrase. I knew immediately that it would change my life. I knew I had spent years and years resisting things, which somehow managed to go right on existing regardless of my refusal to accept them.

If something is, it is. Not to accept it is to live in denial, to remain trapped in resistance by our own choosing. The simple fact is this: whatever exists is completely independent of the stance we take toward it.

There is nothing unworthy of acceptance. It's about as close to a universal truth as we'll ever find. If a murder has been committed, if the planet is toxic, if twenty thousand people starve to death every single day, no amount of furious resisting is going to change any of that. If my parents didn't love me, if I'm a drug addict, if I'm overweight or underpaid, refusing to accept these facts will only lead to a lifetime of make believe.

Before going any further, it's time to make a vital distinction. To accept something because it exists is not at all the same as making it "okay." We put murderers in prison, prosecute gross polluters, and fund international relief agencies to deal with hunger. Similarly, we attempt to heal our personal wounds, recover from self-destructive behavior, and formulate a healthy self-esteem.

If something strikes you as wrong, as ripe for positive change, by all means throw yourself into making it better. But let's take a moment to examine how you might do that. If you're resisting it and are therefore locked up in contraction, the vast portion of your life energy will be unavailable for the effort. If you accept it, however, and allow yourself to expand into the truth of its existence, then your endeavor will immediately benefit from a balanced and flowing commitment.

In my own life, I learned the truth of this all too well. I was one of those kids born with a protest sign in his hand. I found many things in this world truly intolerable. Everywhere I turned there was another cause, another injustice, and with every sighting I grew more and more resistant.

As a young adult, I spent countless hours in political campaigns. Inside, I always felt awful, destroyed by the truth of a world I couldn't accept. Consequently, the way I fought for my causes was pinched, strident. Soon I burned out, as anyone would from living with so much constant contraction.

Had I known at that time that it was possible to accept all I was resisting, I would have been much a happier and more effective activist. In addition, I could have sustained my efforts indefinitely and avoided burnout altogether.

Acceptance does not mean capitulation, nor does it suggest mushy good vibes. Sometimes the state of things fills us with rage, with righteous indignation. It's as important to accept this as it is anything else. And the moment we accept it, we allow for the possibility of expansion. In an expanded state, the anger may or may not remain. But expansive anger, when present, is a thousand times more empowering than the malignant, contracted variety.

There is nothing unworthy of acceptance. The door that sticks, the rash that won't go away, the neighbor's loud music - all of it is here whether we like it or not. Until the day we die, the world will be full of things that we would rather just go away. But their power over us is only commensurate with our resistance. When we stop resisting, we're free to expand. Once expanded, we have infinite resources to change our situation.

Sometimes the change is external. From a place of love and strength, we can oppose an evil and emerge triumphant. The recent demise of apartheid is a good example. But other times such a victory is impossible. Imagine being a slave or a prisoner in one of Hitler's death camps. In such a ghastly circumstance, one has almost no external control. Yet we always have a choice to resist or accept.

There are numerous stories of blacks and Jews who accepted their fates, expanded into limitless love, and served as a beacon for those around them. Some sang, some fought, some merely held up their heads. In each instance, however, they opened to the life force and let it roar mightily through them.

I'd like to close this chapter with a deeply personal story. I'll return to it later in greater detail. It began when I was playing my weekly basketball game. The door to the gym opened and my friend entered. From the look on her face I knew something was terribly wrong.

I left the game and approached her. In a voice hoarse with emotion, she told me that my wife had just attempted suicide. The paramedics found her without any time to spare, and she was now teetering on the brink of death in the intensive care ward of our local hospital.

This happened *after* I'd been graced with bliss. Even still, as I rushed to the hospital, my palms were sweaty, my heart was racing, and my mind was spinning like crazy. Then, something in me began to shift. I noticed my resistance to what was happening. I felt the contraction that had brought it about.

I let out a sigh. I accepted everything. The woman I loved more than anyone in the world might die at any moment. Furthermore, at least some part of her wanted that. This was true whether I could deal with it or not. I expanded into that truth and felt the fundamental bliss of existence surge right back into my being.

By the time I arrived at the hospital, while still intensely concerned, I was at peace with whatever may come. As a result, I became a calm and powerful advocate at a time when my wife needed me most. For both of us, this was the gift of acceptance. And it might have helped save her life.

CHAPTER 8

Awareness

THE DISTANCE BETWEEN RESIS-
tance and acceptance is as vast as galaxies. Yet it's also as near as
the next breath. The first step is the most challenging but requires no movement whatsoever. All that is needed is to bring
our resistance into awareness.

Awareness. A widening of immediate experience that allows
us to detach from resistance long enough to recognize it. "I'm an
alcoholic." "I hate my job." "I can't stand the taste in my mouth."

The recognition of resistance resonates throughout our whole
being. We feel it physically, emotionally. It provides an initial
and tiny expansion, but the space it creates seems huge. The first
time it happens is a revelation. With practice, it can grow into a
sacred habit.

Discussing awareness this way might make it sound easy. No
such luck. The adhesive that binds us to resistance is as powerful
as it is invisible. And the more vital our need to detach, the less
likely it is to release. Sometimes, it seems, our very survival is
dependent upon *not* detaching, upon holding on for dear life to
exactly where we are.

While writing this book, for example, I'm between jobs and
my savings are dwindling. I've got many other irons in the fire,

but nothing's yet taken shape. Every once in awhile I start to panic. I feel my body contracting and my breath growing shallow. I start thinking in circles about my predicament. "What will I do? I can't live this way! I've got to make something happen!"

In those moments, if there's even a glimmer of dawning awareness, the rest of me wants to snuff it out. "This isn't resistance," I might hear myself thinking. "This is real! This is my life! Fancy thinking is not going to put a dime in my pocket! I've got to *do* something!"

When I'm affixed to my resistance with such crazy glue, I'm blinded to the obvious. All of my panic is not about doing anything. It's about refusing to accept what is real. I'm short on funds, temporarily, and whether I feel blissful or miserable doesn't change that.

When I'm able to gain awareness and detach, the reality of my condition is just there. I'm free to see it with greater clarity. And if I follow that awareness to full acceptance, to renewed expansion, then the quality of my effort is bound to improve.

This happens in a very direct way, without fail, no matter the person or the challenge. Expansion fills us with productive energy, keeps us grounded, allows us to focus on what matters most. As a result, it increases our capacity and effectiveness. We work smarter but not any harder.

It occurs to me, after describing my situation, that it might give you pause. You may wonder why you're reading a book about bliss by a guy who hasn't got it made. Though it's tempting to list all my past accomplishments, in this case they're not really relevant. The real answer, as touched upon earlier, is that bliss has nothing to do with external conditions. It doesn't come from any amount of worldly success. It's available right now, to virtually all people, regardless of their station in life.

So far, we've looked at the natural processes of contraction and expansion. We've seen how contraction, which limits our access to bliss, is needlessly prolonged by resistance. This resistance, it turns out, can be counteracted by acceptance. To bring this about, we seek to become aware that we are, in fact, resisting. Once this occurs, once that small but crucial distance has been placed between ourselves and our resistance, then we're ready for the next step home.

The First Try

IT IS OFTEN SAID THAT WE TEACH the things to others we most need to learn ourselves. Must be true, I figure, after what I went through in the writing of this chapter.

It was unusually difficult to get started. I wondered if I would ever pick up steam. Then, finally, everything began to flow. I lost track of time. The distractions around me all receded as the points I wanted to make fell swiftly into place. Soon I was done, thrilled, ready to celebrate…then I hit the wrong key on my computer.

In a split second, the whole chapter was obliterated, deleted. In that same split second, I went from profound expansion to gut-wrenching contraction. This couldn't be happening! It was impossible! First of all, I'm good with computers. Second of all, today's sophisticated software includes redundant backup systems. When you think your file is gone, it's almost always still retrievable.

Almost always. Not this time.

For the better part of an hour, I raged against the machine. My temples pulsed. My jaw clenched. I held my body in rigid, contorted postures as I read the help file a dozen times. I kept looking for that hidden phrase, that glorious instruction, that would end all this agony and bring my chapter back to life.

I hissed at a friend who tried to soothe me. I sniped at the tech support guy when he confirmed the inevitable. Gradually, the truth sunk in. I could resist no longer. Chapter 9 was gone forever.

The Second Try

IT'S NO MYSTERY HOW I TEM-
porarily lost my connection to bliss. The experience of the deleted chapter is a textbook example of contraction and resistance.
I contracted against an unwanted occurrence and then remained
so due to my resistance. After awhile I gained an awareness of my
resistance but still held onto it. Remarkable as it seems, I actually
chose resistance over bliss.

Remarkable as it seems, most of us do that *all day long*.

Eventually, however, I came to my senses. I began the simple
process that would quickly restore me to bliss. That process was,
and is, the topic of both chapter 9s.

It begins with a simple yet revolutionary question...

What is happening right now?

Once we're aware of our resistance, asking this question is
the key to dissolving it.

What is happening right now? Often, the first answers that come
are full of venting. In my case it went something like this — "The
computer stole my work! Technology is evil! It saves time but

exacts a horrible price! I'm ruined! I lost my flow! I'll never finish the damn book!"

These first answers are usually about blaming. In this instance it's the computer's fault, but the culprit could just as easily be oneself, a partner, a parent, a child, a friend, a boss, fate, or even God.

Once the venting runs its course, which grows quicker and quicker with practice, it becomes possible to listen for a truer response. *What is happening right now?* "I deleted my file by accident. It's not retrievable. I'm angry, and frustrated. I tried my best to undo the mistake but it didn't work."

This seems like a pretty accurate description of the situation. Which allows for the second, companion question…

Can I be with it?

To be with something means we accept it as real. We sink into the undeniable truth of what is. This doesn't imply that it will remain forever or that we can't strive to change it, but first, before anything else, we need to fully acknowledge what is happening.

Answering "yes" to this second question produces an immediate unclenching. It allows the resistance to dissipate, the contraction to release. If our "yes" isn't just knee-jerk, if it's a full and visceral acceptance, then expansion won't be far behind.

In the case of chapter 9, when I was finally ready to answer "yes" to the second question, I felt my frustration unravel like yarn in a kitten's paws. Soon I was laughing at the awfulness of what had happened. I wasn't denying it or attempting to minimize it, but instead I was embracing it so completely that it seemed to just disappear.

In fact, what disappeared was my resistance. Which points to a crucial discovery. *What happens in our lives is almost never the source of greatest anguish*. It's our *response*, our *resistance*. And with a little focus and two simple questions, most often we can cease that resistance immediately.

Sometimes the release leads to an outcome even better than we'd imagined in the first place. There is not a more effective way I could have depicted this process than by living through it myself. The final chapter 9 clearly benefited from my misfortune. It doesn't always work like that, of course, but it doesn't need to either.

Most of the time we contract and resist long before the story is over. We gird ourselves needlessly against something ongoing or impending. With the deleted file, I could have asked the two questions much earlier, even right after hitting the wrong key. After a quick sigh or scream, it was entirely possible for me to accept the situation completely. I still might have spent the same hour trying to undo it, but it sure would have been much more pleasant.

The choice was totally mine in that moment, which is true for all of us in every moment. It doesn't matter what happened hours, days, or years ago. In the eternal present, right now, there is always a new chance to gain awareness, to address the two questions, and to open fully to bliss.

CHAPTER 10

Out of the Blocks

AS WE LEARN TO SENSE OUR resistance and begin to ask the two questions, the experience can prove truly exhilarating. We come to see that there is a gold mine of expansion just waiting for us to stake our claim. We approach each new day like prospectors, sifting through life's sediment moment by moment.

In answering the question *What is happening right now?* we uncover resistance to almost everything imaginable. A backache, a stain, our appearance, pollution, the news — all of it can lock us up. When people don't listen, when they hurt our feelings, when they abandon or reject us, we shut right down. In each case, if we ask *Can I be with it?* and the answer is "yes," then the treasure is immediately ours. Regardless of what happens "out there," acceptance enriches *us*.

Sometimes, beginning to ask the questions has the opposite effect. Realizing the extent of our contractions can prove frightful and dispiriting. The gold mine, from this angle, seems more like a bottomless pit. To avoid this, it helps to come out of the blocks slowly, deliberately. Rather than overdoing the questions, we start with small issues and give them plenty of time. For example:

What is happening right now?

> My stomach's full, but I'm still eating. I'm resist-
> ing the fact that my body doesn't want any more
> food because my mind still does.

Can I be with it?

> I don't know. Does that mean I have to stop?

This common situation is illustrative in two ways. First, as
evidenced by the answer to question number two, sometimes we're
not sure we want to stop resisting. Even though the benefits of
expansion are obvious, we can lose sight of them in the rush of
the moment. Second, and especially important, it's easy to assume that letting go of resistance requires us to change our behavior.

In fact, *letting go of resistance requires nothing else whatsoever*. If we're
feeling full, as in the above example, and allow ourselves to accept that fullness, then we become free either to stop eating or
keep going. There is no right or wrong decision implied, no vigilance necessary. Without resistance to impede us, we *are* able to
make a more conscious choice. And that consciousness, over time,
can help free us from unwanted habits.

Once we accept what's happening, we may take just one more
bite. Or two or three. And if we are not able to accept what is
happening, perhaps until *after* the food is all gone, we just begin
whenever we're ready.

Let's continue our example with an all too usual outcome.

What is happening right now?

> My stomach hurts. Why did I keep eating? I'm so stupid. I have no self-discipline. And it didn't even taste that good!

What is happening right now?

> I'm angry at myself. I wish I had made a different choice.

Can I be with it?

> Yeah, I guess. The anger *and* the stomachache. Next time, I hope, I'll stop resisting a lot earlier.

You'll notice, in this case, that the venting is self-directed. You will also notice that the process results in a rather subdued expansion, falling short of any all-out bliss. This brings up a crucial point. At the beginning, when working with the questions is unfamiliar, moments of bliss may prove elusive. If we expect them to be constant and automatic, we'll soon grow frustrated and give up the effort.

There are many reasons why bliss may not always be accessible right away. We'll discuss them in the next section, *Advanced Bliss*, particularly in chapter 18. Two obstacles, however, require some immediate attention.

CHAPTER 11

Stumbling

ASKING THE QUESTIONS RE-
connects us to ourselves. What we find isn't always pleasant. Especially early on, the answers may cause us to stumble. They may
elicit rage, hurt, fear, frustration, confusion, or depression.

For awhile, in fact, things may get worse before they get better. If so, we usually encounter a pair of obstacles. The first might
look something like this:

What is happening right now?

> My best friend just insulted me. No big deal. He
> must be having a hard day.

What is happening right now?

> I'm resisting how bad it feels. I mean I'm sick to
> my stomach.

Can I be with it?

> Something's wrong. This isn't me. One little com-
> ment and suddenly…

What is happening right now?

> I'm all jumbled up. Angry and sad and raw. He's

made similar cracks before, sure, but it never felt
like this.

Can I be with it?

What's the point? It's too much. If this is living
the questions, forget it.

Such a flood of difficult emotion can be so strong, so threat-
ening, that it seems we're about to drown. It's tempting, a la the
Little Dutch Boy, to put a finger in the dike to keep it from crumbling.

The storm's sudden appearance, however, is actually an illusion. Most of these feelings, like our subject's response to previous
insults, have been with us all along. Due to our resistance we have
remained oblivious. Now, the forecast is distorted by fear. If we
can summon up the courage to pull that finger out, to let the emotion flow, the tide won't even begin to submerge us. What seems
like a deluge, in truth, will turn out to be a swimmable stream. And
swimming that stream, thankfully, is exactly what leads to bliss.

While this first obstacle was about the depth of our experience, the second one is about its breadth. Often, when asking
the questions, the answers tumble out in an associative chain. For
instance:

What is happening right now?

There's a five mile backup on the freeway. I'm late

for work. On the worst possible day!

Can I be with it?

No! My clients are already waiting.

What is happening right now?

I'm out of a job, is what's happening! My boss has been salivating for a screwup like this. She's hated me from the moment I started.

Can I be with it?

No! I've had it with her. She's just like my girl-friend. Ever since we started dating, nothing I do is ever good enough.

What is happening right now?

This is ridiculous. Why am I asking these questions? They're just making me more tense.

At a point like this, borrowing from a different legend, it can feel like we've opened up Pandora's Box. Trying to embrace the experience of a mere traffic jam, our subject comes face to face with more serious issues about work and relationship. It's common, when asking the questions, to uncover such multiple resistance. It's equally common to slam the box shut. But what an opportunity missed, since right there, just beneath the tantrum, often lie invaluable discoveries.

What is happening right now?

> My body's in knots. I'm spinning out. I'm sweating, on edge. This traffic is driving me nuts.

Can I be with it?

> I guess I don't have a choice. The whole thing's out of my control.

What is happening right now?

> It seems like when I stop fighting the traffic, there's a bit of inner relief. The panic is still there, but it's not so overwhelming.

What is happening right now?

> I'm noticing how much anger came out about my boss. And my girlfriend, too. I wonder what that's all about.

Can I be with it?

> Maybe, but not right now. It's enough being with all this tension.

Here, continuing to ask the questions leads to a vital awareness of the contraction's *physical* component. Without that, it is often impossible to open further. But once our subject does, the gift of expansion is immediately bestowed. Then, it's possible to acknowledge the additional resistance, to keep the lid open, to let anything and everything fly out.

Emptying the box, at times, is an excruciating proposition. The contents can strike us full-on, wound us with sharp edges. It can seem like we're just gluttons for punishment. But this, too, is an illusion. There is always less in the box than it seems. Plus, the emptier it becomes, the more space we have for bliss.

At the end of the last example, our subject decides not to investigate everything that comes up. That may seem like renewed resistance, but in fact it's perceptive caution. Often, the current situation is too demanding, too fraught. Waiting for a quieter moment can enhance the process. Impatience, on the other hand, can just lead to more contraction.

One contraction at a time is a pretty good general rule. But rules and guidelines are less important than learning what works best for you. Before we move on, it's important to stress that asking the questions and accepting the answers is a deeply personal experience. It's best not to look outside, to a system or a person, for validation that you're doing it "right." What is right in one case is often wrong in another.

It can also be hazardous to weigh your experience against other people's. If they seem less adept than you, it's easy to stiffen with pride. If they seem more skilled, self-doubt and despair are bound to flourish. Truth is, smooth sailing isn't always what's called for. Sometimes we *need* to flounder, or even sink temporarily. What looks like perfect bliss on the outside may actually be a stagnant rut.

Over time, you'll come to trust yourself more and more. Soon, we'll explore some techniques to help strengthen that trust. For now, the important thing is to practice the questions, again and again, to get so comfortable with them that they become second nature. If this starts to seem daunting, like too much work, ask them once in awhile when nothing is troubling you at all. You may find, to your surprise, that "nothing" becomes suddenly sweet.

CHAPTER 12

The Art of Asking

WHEN WE MAKE IT PAST THE
Dutch Boy dilemma and the Pandora problem, our commitment
to the questions begins to solidify. Instead of continuing to wonder if they're worth asking, we are now ready to increase their
effectiveness. To do this, we must learn more about how to ask.
We must learn more, especially, about how not to. In particular,
we need to explore three ways of asking that can cleverly disguise our resistance — analyzing, judging, and bargaining.

ANALYZING

Analyzing occurs when we employ the questions to find an
explanation of the current situation. More than *what*, we strive to
know *why*. This type of asking almost always yields an historical
or theoretical answer.

What is happening right now?

I'm fighting with my boyfriend again. Same old
pattern. Reliving the relationship with my father.

Whether or not this woman's statement is true, it is an interpretation of the moment, an *idea* about what is happening. And an idea, by its very nature, can allow us to distance ourselves from what is.

Almost always, when we respond to the question this way, it's because we have a secret desire to change what is. From the explanation, we hope, will follow a solution. Inherent in this approach is a leapfrogging over acceptance. It defeats the whole purpose of the question. Instead, we need to ask the question in a way that will accept whatever answer comes.

What is happening right now?

> We're fighting again. I'm scared he'll leave. There's a sick, hollow feeling in my chest. The louder he yells, the smaller I feel.

This time, the woman's answer is much more about her *experience*. Instead of a map she visits the actual territory. Now she's got lots to be with. She can be with the fact that her partner might leave. She can be with her fear. She can be with her reaction to rage. In addition, if she chooses, she can keep asking the questions and taking it further.

It's important to note that there's a vital place and purpose for asking conceptual questions. It's not my intention to negate or diminish them at all. But the type of asking that unlocks the present moment for us, that quickly replaces resistance with expansion, is of a different type entirely. It allows us to identify the raw data of the moment and to bathe that moment with attention.

JUDGING

Another common type of misguided asking is the veiled judgment. It assumes that the reason for asking the question in the first place is because something is wrong. Once the "problem" is identified, the logic goes, it can be rooted out quickly and the present moment can return to its blissful state.

When our focus is directed outward, this type of asking produces a response like my tirade against technology. When our focus is inward, which can be far more subtle, it produces a wellspring of self-criticism. Let's imagine the same woman, in the same situation, approaching the argument in just such a manner.

What is happening right now?

> I'm not being assertive enough. He's walking all over me. How many fights and failed relationships is it going to take for me to stand my ground?

This type of self-assessment may or may not be accurate, but from our standpoint it is definitely treacherous. It usually harbors the following deep belief — "The present moment would be absolutely perfect if I could just change the flaws in *myself*." It offers no room to look around, to get comfortable. By overlaying the moment with judgment, it actually *prevents* acceptance instead of promoting it.

In a moment where self-criticism is *already* happening, and the question is asked matter-of-factly, the simple answer might be "I'm criticizing myself." A fuller answer might also include, "There's a sour feeling in my gut, and a stiffening in my shoulders." Prior to asking the question, as we've noted, there's often no awareness of such bodily sensations. With the answer and with full acceptance, they may disappear right along with the resistance.

As before, it's important to add a cautionary note. Just as there is a place for everything else in this world, there is certainly one for vigorous self-examination. Identifying our shortcomings and striving to improve them is certainly a laudable activity. However, it's bound to be a useless effort if the whole enterprise is rooted in contraction. Self-help while contracted is like stepping on a hose and then commanding the water to flow. All our good intentions are automatically canceled out.

BARGAINING

Our final type of counterproductive asking is the bargain. Bargaining begins with the assumption that if we really tell the truth about what we are experiencing, especially when it's difficult, then that experience will go away. We're willing to feel and embrace the present, to really sink into it, if that's what it takes to make the present change.

The bargaining approach is a little more devious than analyzing or judging because it makes a big show of acceptance. It seems to be following the plan. It even seems like there's a superior commitment to the process, a desire to root out ever more difficult truths.

Perhaps the best example in this case is myself. For many years, unconsciously, I was particularly adept at this ruse. I seemed like such a good therapy client, and meditator, and partner in couples counseling, precisely because I reached deep for the most powerful insights. With each new discovery there was a corresponding sense of relief. Sometimes it was the relief of finally understanding, but more often it was because I thought I wouldn't have to feel bad anymore.

Accept the present, goes the formula, and then the present will magically transform itself into something much more appealing. Upon closer inspection, though, this isn't acceptance at all. It begs the question — Would we be willing to accept the present if it *never* changed? If not, then that means our acceptance is conditional. And conditional acceptance is nothing more than disguised resistance.

What is happening right now? Asking the question as a bargain, ironically, *guarantees* that the present will always disappoint us. It creates wonderful answers to our first question yet a resounding "No" to our second.

Can I be with it? Can I be with my current reality no matter how bad it is and no matter how long it lasts? Unless the answer to our second question is a resounding "Yes," then all our work with the first one is meaningless.

"Wait a minute," you might object. "I thought you said that full acceptance leads to bliss. But now you're saying I still have to accept the present if there's no bliss. You're even saying I have to accept it if it's filled with endless misery. But why would I want to do that? What's the point?!"

CHAPTER 13

The Point

A GREAT SPIRITUAL TEACHER once remarked that only three things can happen if we practice meditation. Our lives will get better, worse, or stay the same. Great as he is, the teacher was lying.

The meditative process bears many similarities to the one I'm describing here. And the truth is, if you really devote yourself to it, meditation will only make your life better. So why would the teacher soft sell it? Why would he diminish our expectation from the outset?

The answer is that you cannot liberate the grace in any moment as long as you're trying to. It's another version of stepping on that hose. If you meditate to improve your life, the deepest benefits of the practice will always elude you. If you ask *What is happening right now?* and *Can I be with it?* for the purpose of experiencing bliss, whatever bliss you find will surely be short-lived.

The paradox here is that we encounter bliss only by *not* trying. The more we try, the harder we step on the hose. This is maddening for most people to contemplate, especially Westerners, who are used to achieving objectives through grit and determination. To us, not trying is the same as giving up. Not trying is surrendering.

The word "surrender" can cause much confusion. In relation to a goal it means losing. In a religious context it means recognizing the totality of God's will. In practical terms it refers to the division between what we can and can't control. Used this way, it helps us separate effort from result.

For example, I'm trying very hard to write this book well. I pore over the paragraphs, search for just the right words. But whether or not I succeed in captivating individual readers is something mostly out of my hands. My limits as a writer come into play, as does the particular taste of each person. Understanding this helps me to focus, to give it my all and then let go. Surrendering to the realistic limits of our power isn't about giving up. Instead, it's an essential aid to presence. In addition, it allows us to remain expanded when things don't work out.

For our purpose here, I'd like to submit one final definition. Surrender, to me, is a synonym for full acceptance. There's nothing at all passive about it. It's an active, engaged, productive brand of not trying. It means being with what's happening right now *regardless of what happened before or is about to happen next.* Surrender to the present moment always makes perfect sense. Why? Because there's no possible way to change it.

There is no way to change the present moment. Kick that around awhile. Truly take it in. Doesn't it make resistance seem futile?

In the previous chapter, I wondered which of us would be willing to accept the present moment even if it never changed. That's an important question, but it's also a little misleading. The fact is, every single moment we experience is different from the last. The present is constantly changing, on its own and with no help from us. And whatever changes *we* strive to make in this moment can only show up in future moments.

The point of all this is that acceptance *does* always lead to expansion. Expansion *does* provide access to bliss. The act of asking *What is happening right now?* and then surrendering to the answer is a way of ensuring that access. It's also bound to improve the future, because bliss is such a powerful and positive force. But this improvement, unlike most others, is completely effortless. It will happen over and over, for the rest of our lives, and all we have to do is step off the hose.

CHAPTER 14

Living the Questions

IN THE LAST CHAPTER WE UN-
covered the futility of seeking bliss in the present moment. We
saw how bliss can only come from not seeking, not trying. Now
it's time to explore the actual experience of not trying, to learn
how it looks and feels.

First off, it's important not to control the process in any way.
Therefore, we avoid looking for a particular answer. *"What is happening right now?"* is not the same as "Why is my arm hurting?" or
"What's all this anger about?" The arm or the anger may spur the
question, but if they're part of the asking then the answer will be
unduly bound. In truth, they may just be a side effect of something we're not yet aware of.

With time, it becomes clear that the answers are already there,
always, and that our only job is to wait for them patiently.

Waiting patiently for nothing in particular can feel awkward
and foolish. Just as nature abhors a vacuum, so do our minds.
They're ever-ready to rush in and fill the silence with thoughts,
to agitate the stillness. Resistance, unfortunately, can thrive on
this agitation. It uses all our thinking like a smoke screen, staving
off its impending discovery.

The result is a dangerous trap. Our inclination, because we

want to succeed, is to chastise the mind and demand that it stop sabotaging our effort. But this just creates new resistance on top of the old. Instead, we must file an accurate report.

What is happening right now?

Thinking.

Once the report is filed, we return immediately to the question. If it keeps happening, we keep reporting it faithfully.

The more we resist this habitual vacuum-filling, the more it will increase. The more we allow it to be present, without objection or rebuke, the quicker it will settle down.

If we make it past the mind's roadblock, if we detach from all its trying, something inevitably bubbles up through the stillness. Remember, in most cases we're asking the question because we've become aware of a contraction. We're looking for the resistance that's allowing that contraction to linger.

The good news is that whatever arises naturally, effortlessly, turns out to be exactly what we're resisting. If we're not analyzing or judging or bargaining, there won't be any wrong answers to sift through. In addition, we can authenticate the answer instantly. On a gut level, without any work whatsoever, we automatically know that it's right.

If this seems a little mysterious, it shouldn't. Contraction is never quiet or subtle. It's nature is to scream "Notice me!" over and over until we do. Without benefit of our awareness, however, reality and resistance remain locked in a mutual stranglehold. But the moment we turn toward them, minus any fight of our own, they separate and stand at attention.

"Oh, now I get it! I've been resisting the fact that my husband cheated on me. My arm hurts because I've been walking around with a clenched fist. I'm angry at everyone else because I haven't let myself be angry at *him*."

Once we can fully grasp what caused our contraction in the first place, and what our resistance has made it impossible to see, there's usually another attempt to try, to do something, to make this whole question asking thing worthwhile.

"Now that I've accepted the truth, it's time to move on. I'll throw him out and file for divorce. I'll get a better paying job so money won't be a problem. I'll join a networking group to meet single men."

Using a new realization to forge our next battle plan is another trap. It's a way out of feeling the anger or any other emotion that we contracted against in the first place. Our only job, just as before, is to *keep waiting patiently*. Eventually, the contraction releases and the emotion flows. No matter how bad it feels, no matter how much it hurts, there's no shortcut through the process. But when it's over, at least the first rush, we're in a much better place to plan. In fact, plans often arise unbidden. And we can be confident now that whatever path we choose is not still tainted with resistance.

For the woman in the above example, leaving her marriage may indeed be the right thing. Or, she might decide to give it another chance. But either way, if she'd acted too early, resistance would've ruled the day.

When we ask what's happening in a humble, noninvasive manner, the answer arrives with a clarity never available if we demand it.

Likewise, when we keep asking and accepting, asking and accepting, our resistance fades with a finality never available if we rush it.

It's all about staying open, receptive, committing ourselves to continual surrender. Surrender, we come to learn, is like a muscle. The more we work it, the stronger it grows. The stronger it grows, the more present we become.

This is what the poet Rilke meant, I believe, when he commanded us to "live the questions." And living the questions, it turns out, is a practical invitation to bliss.

CHAPTER 15

Perfect Poison

What is happening right now?

I'm thinking about my friend who just bought a big new house.

He irritates me. I'm feeling irritated.

Who does he think he is, spending all that money when so many people are suffering?

I'm feeling resentful. Why should he have all that while I have nothing at all? It's not even about hard work. I work just as hard as he does. He got lucky, that's all.

I'm feeling unlucky. I'm holding my breath and tightening my jaw.

What's wrong with life? What's wrong with me?

I feel ashamed, humiliated. I hate feeling ashamed and humiliated. I'm resisting feeling ashamed and humiliated. Whoa! That must be true, because just saying it feels like swallowing poison.

What is happening right now?

> Thinking about my friend's good fortune has brought me face to face with my own *mis*fortune. Hard as it is to accept, I'm a poor, unlucky failure.

Can I be with it?

> Do I have to? Why can't I just keep resenting my friend and avoiding my own experience?

What is happening right now?

> I'm angry. I don't want to feel this! I'm contracting around the pain of being a total failure.

Can I be with it?

> I don't know. If I let that feeling wash over me, if I don't attempt to shield myself from it, does that mean it'll go away? Will I get to stop feeling like a total failure?

What is happening right now?

> I'm bargaining instead of surrendering. I'm afraid to surrender to the feeling of total failure.

Can I be with it?

> Well… I don't know. Maybe I can give it a try.

What is happening right now?

The fear is huge. I can't stand it! I feel like it's going to suffocate me. Why the hell am I doing this? It's agony.

But...wait... It's starting to subside a little. Yeah, it's moving to the background now.

Can I be with it?

Can I be without the fear of feeling like a total failure?! Sure.

What is happening right now?

Let me see. Oh, right. I'm still feeling like a total failure.

Can I be with it?

I guess. My God — it's like a punch in the gut. I feel like I'm going to throw up.

Useless. Good for nothing.

This is even worse than the fear! Help! It's like I'm falling apart. Disappearing.

But...at the same time there's another feeling. It's kind of...a relief. There's a freedom in just letting it be there. I feel free. Still a little ravaged, but free.

What is happening right now?

I'm not fearful *or* resistant anymore. I'm just hanging out with this failure thing, living it, watching
it. It's not really me, though. I mean there's a part
of me which feels that way, but just a part. The
rest of me feels, well, okay.

This sample inner dialogue is a more detailed approximation
of what happens when we begin asking the two questions in earnest. Many of the answers actually come as feelings and sensations, rather than words. They're verbalized here only out of ne-
cessity. In fact, the questions themselves soon become habitual
and are asked at a deeper level than language. Living the questions, over time, supplants the need to articulate them.

With those caveats, let's take a look at the example. In the
beginning, asking the first question leads to a jumble of thoughts
and feelings, external judgments and internal reactions. There's a
real desire to learn the answer but also a churning, defensive posture. This mixture of willingness and resistance is typical, even
vital. It marks the shift into *fertile awareness*. Fertile awareness lets
us know that we're in the right place, that this is where we need
to grow. The friction we feel is what tills the soil. It makes room
for true answers to spring forth.

When the true answer springs forth in our example — a sense
of shame and humiliation — it produces a stunning blow. This is
the *proof of authenticity* described in the last chapter, the way we
automatically know an answer's right. It can come quickly or
slowly. Until it occurs we keep repeating the first question. You

may have spotted this repetition earlier, in our example about the traffic jam. You'll find it happens naturally in your own practice. After all, it's no use asking yourself to be if you don't yet know what to be *with*.

Sometimes the proof of authenticity is an easy, quiet knowing. But more often than not, especially when there's lots of resistance, it's a bitter pill to swallow. In our current example the subject gags a few times, first on resistance, next on bargaining, and then on the fear of letting all that go. Accepting the fear that emerges is a necessary precursor to accepting what the fear's about. There's no way around the fear, just as there's no way around the resistance. But wading through fear is half the journey, and the release it provides is a tasty motivation to continue.

When left face to face with the feeling of failure, the original source of contraction, our subject wavers a moment and then takes a courageous dive. Soaking in a sense of utter worthlessness, actually *being* worthless, can produce a shattering kind of pain. Many people find the experience so intolerable that they'll turn to drugs, crime, abusive relationships — anything to blunt the blow.

The same is true of all excruciating emotion. To resist it is nearly automatic. To accept it, no matter how great the eventual reward, is almost always a grudging endeavor.

Luckily, our subject perseveres. What results is a priceless reward. The sense of worthlessness rises, crests, and recedes. The contraction washes right away with it. In the wake of the wave things are fresh, renewed, full of possibility. Where once there was rigidity and stagnation, now there's expansion and flow.

This example points out a key cost of resistance. Previously, we saw how the present moment changes constantly, on its own, without any help from us. Resistance, however, can partially stymie this change. It acts like a maximum security prison, incarcerating the unaccepted aspect of reality while everything else marches on. The longer we continue to resist, the more catch-up we ultimately require.

Finally, when we accept what's really happening, it's like a reunion between prisoner and loved ones. The heart pounds, flings open in celebration.

Obviously, every occurrence of this process is unique. Most aren't as swift or tidy as the one above. As we'll discuss later, sometimes contractions unravel in layers, and other times they just release and return, release and return, no matter how many times we ask the questions. In addition they can show up in bunches, compounding the challenge, revealing many different contractions against the same issue.

It can help, when contractions become overwhelming, to ask the questions with a supportive friend. Sometimes an outside perspective is just what we need to cut to the heart of the matter. Make sure, however, that your partners in exploration aren't combative. This often happens with even the best intentions, since it's easy for our friends to see what we can't, or won't, and get frustrated along the way. Though tempting, it never serves to hurry the process, or to force-feed understanding. A confrontational environment, in the end, only produces more resistance.

Whether dissolved in tandem, solo, or not at all, contractions are a part of life. If you're human, you contract. If you're human, you resist. No matter who you are, no matter how exalted, there's no escaping this fate.

Yet, on the other hand, in every moment there's boundless freedom. No matter who you are, no matter how far gone, there's no exception to the rule.

To live in this freedom requires one thing and one thing only. Simple as it seems, and hard as it is, all you have to do is be.

CHAPTER 16

Bill of Goods

MOST OF THE LITERA-
ture of bliss is written by mystics. The mystic vision is remarkably similar across religions, cultures, and centuries. It asserts that
the glory of God is present in every object, every experience,
every being, and every moment. Our job is to pierce the veil of
illusion that keeps us from living this truth. When we do, shattering our egos in the process, a direct perception of divinity suf-
fuses us with radiant bliss. We come to see that all existence has
been created by God, out of God, and that nothing is more or
less divine than anything else. Joy and sorrow, good and evil —
they're equal expressions of All That Is.

This mystical orientation is not the same as pantheism, which
holds that God is present in all things. The latter is a belief, while
the former is said to be an experience, something which happens
to an individual whether invited or not. It's as if being shattered
brings a mystic closer to the source from which all energy springs,
and that from the new vantage point things appear in a state prior
to form, prior to the countless particularities that make up the
world as we know it.

In a state of mystical rapture there is no self and other, no
subject and object. Instead there is only God, or Void, or what-

ever name we give the nameless. Witnesses to this state, attempting to voice what can't be spoken, have nevertheless compiled an
inspiring record of their attempts. There's Rumi the Moslem, St.
Teresa the Christian, Reb Nachman the Jew, and scores of Buddhist and Hindu sages. In each generation new voices emerge.
Our own is full of them, and with like-minded explorers who've
found similar testimonies in lesser known native traditions.

Returning to the source of creation is tantalizing for many.
The suggestion that we might live to tell the tale is almost irre-
sistible. It fuels the use of psychotropic drugs and is said to be the
deepest cause of most addictions. Yet, as we've come to know,
the signature feature of addictions is that they can never deliver
what they promise. Their bill of goods seems too good to be
true, and it is.

Sadly, I believe mystical declarations bear a perilous similar-
ity. The problem isn't that mystics have deliberately misreported
their experience. If anything, their courageous attempts to share
the unshareable are a gift to be treasured. The problem is that
mystics often become so overwhelmed by their taste of divinity
that it's all they describe. Meanwhile the other half of the story,
about their continuing life as human beings, is either relegated to
the background or glorified to the point of irrelevance.

One who is blessed by mystic bliss still has to eat, sleep, go
to the bathroom, and make a living. There might be a monastery
to escape to, which solves some survival issues, but usually such
retreats are just as rife with social conflict as most "real world"
locales. While ecstatic testaments serve to entice and uplift us,

they imply a ceaseless type of rapture that no mortal can ever sustain. It's impossible to be high all the time, whether on ayahuasca or God's grace.

So what does all this have to do with our own investigation of bliss? The answer lies in how we might actually expect to experience it. I began this book with the claim that bliss is ever-available. I still maintain that to be true. But with each contraction that occurs, we unconsciously turn away from bliss. It's available, but not chosen. However, once we've located our contractions, as well as any resistance layered on top of them, we're free to accept all that's been denied and welcome bliss back into the fold.

Once we learn to live the questions, our experience of the present moment is like an alternating current of contraction and expansion, resistance and bliss. With practiced attention, the periods of contraction and resistance grow shorter and shorter, while the periods of expansion and bliss stretch out longer and longer. In addition, the causes of contraction continue to diminish. What once seemed like huge traumas soon come to appear rather trivial. With less to trigger contraction, bliss is much freer to flow.

Living the questions is never about getting "blissed out." Nor is it about abandoning the material world, or everyday consciousness, or the entire realm of embodied experience. Rather, it's about total, unconditional presence. It's about showing up, and opening up, completely. When we're truly ready to do that, with every cell in our bodies, bliss is part of the natural outcome.

Unlike the promise of eternal mystic rapture, this bill of goods isn't too good to be true. It is true. Better yet, it costs nothing and demands no sacrifice. Instead of giving up something, the only requirement is to *accept everything*. Furthermore, all of this can be verified by paying attention to our own lives, just as they are, without subscribing to a belief system or a program or any type of spiritual austerity.

There is no right time to begin asking *"What is happening right now?"* Every time is the perfect time. In the middle of an argument, daydreaming at the office, beset by a sleepless night — each of these common occurrences offers another opportunity to return to the present, to come home.

But perhaps this process of questioning and accepting serves its greatest function when we're stuck, or challenged, or facing one of life's inevitable trials. These are the experiences which cause us to contract the tightest, to resist the hardest.

When we truly hate what's happening, our instinct is to flee from it like a house on fire. But if we can learn to turn around and *enter* that fire, to let it burn all our resistance away, then we find ourselves arising from the ashes with a new sense of power and freedom. If we're able to accept *that*, we come to understand everything else is a piece of cake.

In chapter 7, I touched on the story of my wife's suicide attempt. I wrote about my trip to the hospital and all the fear and anxiety which arose inside me. I described the way that acceptance of all that fear allowed bliss to surge back into my being. What I couldn't communicate then, before laying the foundation in succeeding chapters, was the way that bliss arrived *alongside* all my fear and anxiety.

Throughout my experience at the hospital, I kept asking *"What is happening right now?"* The answer kept coming back, "I'm nervous, terrified." Then I'd ask, *"Can I be with it?"* Thankfully, the answer was consistently "Yes."

Despite this constant awareness of my shaky state and a full acceptance of it, all the fear didn't go away. I felt afraid, then blissful, afraid, then blissful. Sometimes, it seemed, I felt them both at the exact same time.

So there I was, showing up for my life when I could barely tolerate it. What made it tolerable, even more than the bliss, was my rock solid commitment to accept everything, even the parts of me that didn't want to accept *anything*.

This commitment to life, to whatever it brings in the present moment, is the essence of Basic Bliss. It's possible for me, for you, for virtually anyone who's willing.

What is happening right now?

Can I be with it?

Our commitment to vulnerability, in a sublime paradox, is what renders us truly invincible.

* * *

PART THREE

Advanced Bliss

CHAPTER 17

Dissent

Note: This chapter examines the case against bliss. It's an attempt to set forth and rebut the most common critiques. Therefore, it's a bit more abstract and argumentative than the rest of the book. If you've arrived here in sequence and have no serious qualms with what's come before, you might consider just skimming it.

WHEN PRESENTED WITH THE idea that bliss is available to virtually all of us, all of the time, many people tense up instantly. Just the thought of reveling in this bliss feels excessive, sinful, and supremely narcissistic. We're here to serve, these people claim, not gratify our every whim as if we're God. And besides, how can we possibly be blissful when billions live in abject misery and the world around us is crumbling?

Let's refer to this as the Selfish Argument. Since it's probably the most prevalent, we might as well examine it first.

THE SELFISH ARGUMENT

Central to the Selfish Argument is the idea that pursuing bliss comes at the expense of all other pursuits, and particularly those which emphasize humility and duty. But this isn't true at all. As described in Part Two, bliss is a by-product of complete presence and the ability to embrace the contractions and resistances which arise in us from moment to moment. Paying attention to our actual experience of life allows us to step off the hamster wheel of mindless self-gratification. Our willingness to accept everything that arises must especially include all pain and suffering.

This process of total acceptance doesn't require us to change who we are or what we do. Therefore, the bliss that comes with it is just as available to an activist as a monk, and to a communist as a conservative. Bliss is an equal opportunity provider and does not screen candidates on the basis of race, class, sex, belief, or lifestyle.

But what about the sheer limits of our time and focus? Don't we have to choose whether to look within or without? Doesn't continued attention to what's happening in our own experience detract from attention we might be paying to the outside world? And isn't the outside world where we are needed the most?

To this line of questioning I offer the following axiom — *The quality of our external attention is commensurate with the quality of our internal acceptance.* In other words, we can only give to the world around us what we're willing to give ourselves.

Let me offer an extreme example. I know a woman who is a journalist in the Middle East. This woman lives and breathes her beat so thoroughly that she neglects even a rudimentary self-awareness. As a result she's incredibly high-strung, to the point that her skills are seriously affected. Interview subjects respond to her guardedly, or read her insecurities expertly enough to manipulate the process. While this woman has ostensibly dedicated her life to the pursuit of truth, more often than not her limited introspection produces deeply flawed reporting. The outer world she presents is distorted by the inner world she ignores.

In my own case, as touched upon in chapter 4, I was a born radical. Anywhere there were victims in the world, I rose up fiercely in their defense. On the surface this seemed noble, but it lent my crusades a shrill, off-putting quality that seriously hindered their effectiveness.

I often wondered where all this came from, since I had no political role models at all. Only years later, in therapy, did I discover my own hidden hurt. Quickly it became clear that my need to fight for victims was due in large part to repressed vulnerability. I fought all around me what I couldn't bear within me.

Psychologists know this as projection and see it as a universal aspect of the human psyche. Onto the blank slate of the world around us we project the disowned parts of ourselves. This is as true of races and nations as it is of individuals. Usually, with equal blindness, the recipients of those projections do the exact same thing to us. Only by shifting our focus inward, and excavating our personal demons, can we undo this debilitating cycle.

The final piece of the Selfish Argument is both its most emotional and most peculiar. Somehow, for many of us, feeling good in the presence of those who suffer is a guilty pleasure. We judge it unseemly and dim our light out of supposed compassion. But this instinctive response begs the obvious question — when has anyone ever benefited from other people feeling bad? Is the homeless person on the street somehow *wounded* by our joy? Does punishing ourselves with pity help address the root causes of homelessness?

In fact, usually the real reason we feel so rotten around homeless people (or anyone less fortunate) is nothing other than ordinary fear. We recoil from the idea that they could be us. And then, we either rush off with irritation or hastily unload some change. Either way, imprisoned by our own contraction, we turn away from what's really happening.

By contrast, at the core of true bliss is always an expansive love. This love is never selective, or superior. It's not to be flaunted, but neither is it to be hoarded. To accept everything within is precisely what unlocks our hearts and brings us closer to the outside world. And the more we truly embrace the world, the more likely our efforts to heal it will succeed.

As we'll come to see in the following chapters, choosing bliss renders us not selfish, but selfless.

THE CLOUD ARGUMENT

Choosing bliss can sound a lot like living in the clouds. To some it seems passive, escapist, and numbing. In large part we have the 60s to thank for this. The counterculture of that era gave bliss a bad name by tuning in, turning on, and dropping out.

As described above, the bliss that comes from total presence has nothing to do with being laid back. While definitely available to the idle, it is also there to be seized by those who function at any speed. Many people may question this. They may feel too pressured, too overburdened to apply the focus that living the questions requires.

The truth, however, is that after a brief learning curve the process becomes nearly automatic. Most often it happens quickly, naturally, *alongside* all our other activities. Furthermore, a deeper awareness causes our perception of passing events to slow down. What once felt like an intolerable whirlwind soon tempers to a bearable breeze.

Neither is choosing bliss in any way escapist. To accept everything, of course, is to escape nothing. The hippie archetype is indeed escapist, as it denies the darker aspects of life in order to simulate a serene ideal. There's no room in the clouds for ambition, aggression, violence, and evil. But since to some extent these impulses are present in all of us, attempting to banish them is the same as disowning them. After all, clouds cast shadows too.

But what about the numbing claim? Isn't bliss just one color of the emotional spectrum? Wouldn't residing there all the time be reductive, even boring? While this topic is broached at some length in chapters 12 and 16, suffice it to say that the practice of total presence does nothing to diminish one's range of emotion. In fact, it actually broadens and sharpens the spectrum by coaxing into awareness any feelings previously shunned. At the same time, the constant proximity of bliss provides a cushioning effect to life's greatest challenges. And, since bliss increases in proportion to our acceptance, it also acts as an inducement to continue accepting.

THE CLICHÉ ARGUMENT

It's almost a given these days that people who have survived a brush with death or recovered from a serious illness will talk about their renewed pledge to "live in the moment." It is so easy to say, and so often said, that the phrase teeters close to meaninglessness. No wonder, then, that people often ridicule the "be here now" crowd. All of us are richly complicated, they point out, and to suggest that one simple approach to happiness would work for everybody is an insult to the intelligence.

When we show up in the now and pay close attention, what arises, indeed, is infinitely complex. It is about who we are, how we came to be, and just about the whole of history leading up to it. True acceptance of all that means not softening it, not editing it, and definitely not simplifying it.

On the other hand, a great many of life's complications come from *rejecting* the now, from our endless penchant to gird against it and to pretend that life is otherwise.

He doesn't love me. She never listens. I'm sick. I'm lonely. I don't really know who I am.

Cliché or not, what a relief the present can be when we stop running long enough to get acquainted with what drives us crazy. The content, it turns out, is what is specific to each individual. Attendance, however, is the one thing that's always required.

THE HERO ARGUMENT

Isn't it true, this argument goes, that the greatest minds of history, science, and culture propel us forward by their very refusal to accept things as they are? Doesn't rejecting the status quo lead to vision and innovation? If we embrace the grain of sand so fully, how is it ever going to become a pearl?

It would be futile, of course, to rail against the likes of Napoleon, Einstein, or Picasso. And it's widely believed that their various neuroses are inextricably tied to their brilliance. Certainly a blissful Picasso would never paint Guernica. Or would he?

I would suggest that the icon of tortured genius is due for serious review. In my experience, the practice of total presence, and the peace it provides, actually liberates people to become *more* of who they are. I believe that an Achilles who becomes intimate with his heel can then adjust his fighting style accordingly. Indeed, presence might turn out to be his greatest ally.

A famous film director once went to an analyst to uncork his chaotic inner world. He asked the analyst if the process of self-discovery might diminish his creative edge. The analyst, in all candor, agreed it was a possibility. At that instant the director fled, never to return.

The first tragedy in that story is that the director chose professional success over his own happiness. The second tragedy is that we never got to see the films that might have sprung from him in a state of greater wholeness. The third tragedy, and perhaps proof of the previous two, is that after a period of intense success the director plunged into an artistic rut.

THE FUTILITY ARGUMENT

The final argument I'm familiar with begins with the fact that it is impossible to experience bliss all the time. In that case, why does it make any sense to pursue it?

The answer to this is plain and simple. It doesn't. As outlined in chapter 13, to grasp for bliss is to guarantee its absence. Instead, we look to the present moment and dismantle the fortresses we've built there. We engage life instead of combating it. And then, inevitable and miraculous, bliss reveals itself in all we find.

CHAPTER 18

Radar

*A commitment to accept everything
will necessarily bring up everything.*

RECENTLY A FRIEND CALLED TO to tell me she's getting married. I congratulated her with enthusiasm, but there was also a hollow quality to my voice. I don't think she heard it, but I certainly did. Then, hanging up the phone, I noticed a desire to file away the conversation and get back to my own life. The whole thing felt like an annoyance, an unnecessary distraction.

Soon, however, I began to wonder at this response. Why wasn't I all the way there for her? Why did I need to pretend like the whole thing hadn't even happened? Knowing these as telltale signs of contraction, I took time out to live the questions.

Making sure to breathe, I felt a pulling in my diaphragm and a deep furrow in my brow. I leaned into those sensations until my body went soft. I let it become the asking itself. As I waited without straining, the first thing that bubbled into my awareness was that my friend hadn't returned my last phone call. That had made me a little angry. Underneath the anger was a twinge of hurt, and

I saw how her joyous announcement precluded my ability to bring that up. Compared to the engagement, of course, it was a small thing. So why couldn't I just let it go?

In a few more moments I understood. I couldn't let it go because I hadn't let it be. Prior to the call, I had periodically wondered why she had been ignoring me. But before I could feel my emotions about this, I turned them into a judgment about her. "She is flaky and unreliable. I should downgrade her from close friend status."

My resistance to feeling angry and hurt prevented me from accepting the fact that I was angry and hurt. Locked in place, this resistance kept me from being fully present during our phone call. Had I moved through it earlier, I would have been free to bring the issue up right then or save it for another time. Either way the choice would have been mine. Instead, ignorance of my resistance led to an automatic, half-there reaction.

It took a little while for me to absorb all that, to let my mind and body assimilate what I had discovered and feel what I had previously denied. In addition, I had to accept some shame about my inability to catch this quicker, about being anything less than perfect.

All of this acceptance released my contraction about the unreturned phone call. I felt calm, even a little blissful. But at the same time, I also noticed some residual tension. As I left the house for a round of errands, I continued to ask myself what was happening.

Waiting in line at the post office, it came to me. Hearing

about those wedding plans brought up some regret about my divorce. I thought I was through with that. I thought the healing was complete. Yet I wanted to cry out "Hey! You can't get married and live happily ever after! That's what *I* wanted. If it didn't happen for me, then it doesn't get to happen for anyone!"

Again I felt immediate shame, this time for experiencing such envy. But the envy was just a mask for contraction, for a remaining shard of pain that I'd managed to bypass. It was difficult to accept that I was capable of so much bungling. Of course bungling just means being human, so I licked my wounds and headed humbly for the drug store.

Roaming the aisles, picking up some blades for my razor, I grieved a little for the demise of my marriage. I accepted the fact that those wounds might never heal completely and that from time to time I may need to feel their sting. A part of me resisted this idea of a future enslaved by the past — I want to be free! — but soon it, too, expanded back into the here and now.

Later that night, preparing dinner, I started thinking about how hard it is to find lasting relationships. I flashed back to my mother, to all the troubles we had, and to the unhealthy patterns they fostered. For a moment I contracted against this sad reminiscence, but then I had to laugh. This was still about my friend's engagement. One phone call, with nothing but good news, brought up my oldest and deepest issues.

Of course this is how it always is and always will be. A commitment to accept everything will necessarily *bring up* everything. Yet it's misleading to use that term, "bring up," since in fact it's always right there with us. Our only choice is whether to acknowledge it and embrace it and live through it, or deny it and contract against it and let it surreptitiously rule our lives.

Events like that phone call occur so regularly that we don't even notice. It's easy to track the big stuff, like tragedies and great disappointments, but those smaller contractions sneak right under the radar. To catch them all can seem daunting, a never-ending task. Actually, however, there's more than enough time. After all, what usually occupies us at the post office or the drug store? For the most part just mental chatter. The advantage of living the questions is that while it calls for our total presence, it doesn't require anything else. There are no concepts to understand, no problems to solve. As long as we continue to show up, the rest takes care of itself.

CHAPTER 19

Backlog

Locked within our past contractions
are the keys to our future expansions.

HOW DOES "THE REST TAKE care of itself"? Isn't that impossible? If total acceptance in the present simply dissolves all our past contractions, then why do people spend millions of dollars and years of their lives in the pursuit of inner healing?

To answer these questions, let's back up a step. In chapter 15 we looked at how resistance becomes a maximum security prison. We saw that whatever we don't accept when it arises remains locked away inside us. In chapter 17 we examined the process of projection, in which the disowned parts of ourselves cast their shadows into daily life.

It shouldn't be a surprise, by this point, that the prisoner and the projector are one and the same. Contraction is the victim. Contraction is the culprit. Inside every contraction is a wealth of life energy. Its nature is to flow, to transform. It rails against incarceration with everything it has. Projection is the best tool available, so it shines that light like crazy.

Disowned is just another word for unconscious. So unlike

memory, or life lessons, or anything else we carry knowingly from the past, undissolved contraction functions beneath our conscious awareness. It is able to cloud our perspective and manipulate our actions precisely because we don't know it's there. On the other hand, the results of its presence are easy to spot.

COMPULSION

The most reliable sign of old contraction is a pattern of compulsive behavior. It might be overt, like drug abuse, or more subtle like choosing unhealthy relationships. It might even be relatively trivial, like the biting of nails or grinding of teeth. Such self-destruction always feels out of our control. And it is, in fact, as long as contraction is running the show.

But what seems on the surface like punishment is actually a cry for freedom. The original wound, trapped and desperate, is stuck replaying the same old scene. It projects the scene over and over because that's the only one it knows. As long as we turn away or keep fighting against it blindly, the cycle is bound to continue.

I lived out this cycle in my twenties through a string of doomed affairs. Still unaware of my disowned vulnerability, I kept attracting "wounded birds," wonderful but seriously troubled women. I'd fall for each one madly and then hope if I saved her she would return my love. It never worked, of course, and I vowed time and time again to choose more wisely. What didn't occur to me, until much later, was that I wasn't doing the choosing at all.

The longer a contraction stays buried, the more destructive it becomes. The wound inside it is forced to implode. The result is a black hole in the heart, or the gut, and nothing can fill that void. Yet, entrenched as it is, and no matter how old, the wound only craves one thing. Acceptance. With enough consistent acceptance, even the oldest wounds eventually heal.

LIVING THE DEATH

Let's take a look at how that happens. Let's use another sign of old contraction — deep-seated fear. Imagine, for the moment, that you are a person who loves to sing. You do it in the shower and the car but can't bear to perform in public. Actually you would love to, but just the thought of it sends a jolt of terror down your spine.

As you begin to live the questions and the next jolt of terror comes, you decide to yield to it instead of clamping down.

What is happening right now?

I'm thinking about singing onstage. My heart is pounding and my hands are clammy. I feel a little dizzy. There's a frozen feeling, too. It starts in my stomach but spreads out everywhere.

Can I be with it?

No! I want to run and hide, curl into a little ball.

But…I promised myself I'd try something different. So — here goes.

What is happening right now?

…It's overtaking me. In rushes. They're almost unbearable. I'm trembling and cringing and fighting the urge to close up.

Then, a while later:

Wait a minute. It seems to be subsiding. Yeah, it's almost gone now. I feel…wow…like I'm wide open.

Simply being with your long-held fear, after so much resistance, produces a profound relief. There is a sense that you can live through anything. At the same time, however, you're not about to book a nightclub. You wonder why. This wondering sends an invitation.

What is happening right now?

Nothing, really. Just waiting, staying present. Hold on — stuff's coming now. Flashes.

My brother, always making fun of my voice…

That concert in grade school when I forgot the words…

Dad, and that scowl of his. The way he looked right through me whenever I messed up.

Can I be with it?

Why? They're just bad memories. Of course they're what got me here. So what?

It's tempting to quit right there, to turn away from such old news. But it's not information you're after — it's *liberation*. So this time, you grab hold of yourself and stay put. You open to these old contractions like never before.

What is happening right now?

Instead of just thinking about those memories, now I'm starting to *relive* them. It's happening all by itself. Ugh. So much pain.

Can I be with it?

I don't know. It feels like the whole word is judging me, condemning me. Like every inch of my body is diseased and on display. I feel naked, vile. My worst nightmare.

What is happening right now?

This can't be. But, I might as well say it. I feel...I actually feel like I'm dying.

This feeling of impending death defies description. No wonder you've resisted so long. No wonder you won't sing in public, or submit your poems, or hardly ever say what you think.

But now, finally, it's time to *live* that death. So you just sit there, asking the questions over and over. Maybe tears come, or wrenching sobs, or groans of pent-up grief. Still, all you do is sit there. All you do is accept what comes.

In a little while the intensity subsides. You are weary, wrung-out. You haven't really died, of course, yet somehow you feel newly born. Things are beginning to seem fresh, full of promise. Maybe you will book that nightclub, and then again maybe you won't. But either way, from now on, at least it will be *your* decision.

Contractions from the past, especially the formative ones, make everything else look like child's play. To liberate them on our own takes real courage. And, to top it off, they usually don't dissolve in one sitting. Often they require frequent revisiting, and wave after wave of release, to free up all that's been stuck.

Then, on the opposite extreme, some contractions are buried so deeply that years can go by before they surface. In these cases we feel an ominous calm. We grow impatient for things to move.

THE HEALING ARTS

It is no wonder, with all that difficulty, that people turn to outside help. Over the past decades, the methods of assistance have increased tremendously. For those who like it grueling, there

is psychoanalysis. For those who want it now, there is hypno-
therapy. Twelve step programs appeal to our sense of community, while bodywork gets us out of our heads. Meditation culti-
vates a deeper awareness, while healers clear energetic blocks.

The list, of course, goes on and on. Each discipline has its
own subsets, jargon, offshoots, and squabbles. Just sifting through
them can cause contraction, but that's not to say they aren't worthwhile. Many people find them indispensable. From the perspective of total presence, however, they're a decidedly double-edged
sword.

The best of these healing systems help a person find the
present moment and stay there. They hold the space for whatever comes up, and bring perspective to the rough passages. In
addition, they might offer techniques for coaxing contraction into
the light. Finally, they provide companionship and reassurance
along the often lonely road.

How much we benefit from a healing art is determined entirely by how we approach it. If we use it as described above, then
our presence and acceptance increase. But if we use it to mediate
the moment with analyzing, judging, or bargaining, its impact
will be severely limited. And the problem is that it is easy to do.

What a temptation, for example, to learn about a new theory
and then channel the present moment through it. "I'm supporting
my inner child," for example. Or, "I'm acting too codependent."
Often, this type of language removes us a crucial degree from our
experience. There is no *actual* inner child, of course. It is only an
idea. Sometimes, an idea like that can even be a tool for resis-

tance, for abandoning a moment entirely because it doesn't fit the chosen model.

Likewise, suppose we learn about the way contraction accumulates in the body and work with a health professional to loosen up. But then, upon noticing a new contraction, we jump to the conclusion that something is "wrong." Instead of giving the present moment a chance to breathe, we use our new-found understanding to "fix" it.

Maybe the most common way to shirk the present is by fooling ourselves with false commitment. Going to therapy every week, for instance, means nothing without a willingness to accept what arises. But many people use their mere attendance as a way *not* to be there. They will talk about anything and everything except what's really happening. This may even go on for years.

The worst healing approaches make no attempt to defuse these mechanisms of avoidance. In fact they encourage them, offering a wide variety of short-cuts and quick fixes. Truth is, there are two rules about how long each person's process should take. The first rule is that it takes as long as it takes. The second rule is that attempting to deny the first rule always makes it take much longer.

BREAKING THROUGH

Locked within our past contractions are the keys to our future expansions. There's no way in advance to tell how much life energy a contraction contains. It may just carry a small burst, or house an entire part of our personality. Living the questions, without trying to rush the answers, assures we don't miss any gifts.

In addition to analyzing, judging, and bargaining, working with the past leads to one more pitfall. Sometimes, once we open to a contraction, the stories and feelings inside are incredibly alluring. There's so much pain, or essence, or sheer drama that we can't let go. Instead of accepting we begin *wallowing*. Our need to be swept away, unfortunately, just re-traps all that energy. In the end, we trade one type of contraction for another.

Breaking through the backlog completely, though rewarding, puts our presence to the greatest test. Here, especially, things may get worse before they get better. And it dawns on us, over time, that the endeavor is truly lifelong. Some contractions, at least pieces of them, we're bound to take to our graves. Coming to this realization often produces a crisis of faith. "If there is no end," it's fair to ask, "then what is the purpose? And besides, isn't this supposed to be about bliss?"

With the dissolving of each contraction, no matter how small and no matter how partial, comes a simultaneous expansion. Each expansion restores us to the flow of life, and bliss, as ever, is there at the heart of this flow.

Remember, bliss is the result but never the goal. Neither is the goal to be fully healed or free of contraction. The only goal is total presence. In the space of total presence, with or without outside help, past contractions arise on their own. Acceptance, too, arises in the same natural manner.

This acceptance includes the fact that we may analyze, judge, bargain, and wallow. It includes the fact that we might opt for a quick fix. It includes the fact that contraction may always remain. It includes the fact, paradoxically, that sometimes we're *not willing* to accept.

Eventually, we come to see that past contraction is not a problem or an impediment. It simply is, like everything else that is. Just as no moment is "better" or "worse" than another, neither is any amount of contraction.

Staying open to our past contractions turns out to be its own reward. Ultimately there is no crisis of faith, because faith isn't even required. When pondering if it's all worthwhile, our lives become the living proof.

CHAPTER 20

Wiring

*Understanding the role of personality helps us to
live the questions. Living the questions, in turn,
allows us to distinguish between what's fluid and fixed.*

PART OF ACCEPTANCE REQUIRES
letting go. We let go of what we *think* is happening, or what we
wish were happening, so that what's actually happening can make
an appearance. In the beginning, for most of us, this feels odd
and unnatural. We've spent the majority of our lives trying so
hard, pushing against what is, that we overestimate the influence
of our will. We assume that we make life happen. We assume that
we make *ourselves* happen.

Letting go, letting the moment proceed on its own, can feel a
lot like disintegrating. Because we associate so much of our identity with assertion, with doing, surrender to the present seems
like surrender of self. We fear we're committing suicide. If I stop
trying to be myself, the logic goes, I won't be anyone at all.

The terror of dissolution is enough to send many people fleeing from the moment forever. Those who stick around, though,
encounter a surprising discovery. It turns out, upon closer exami-
nation, that being ourselves doesn't require much work. Our

uniqueness, our personality, functions whether we want it to or not. A friend of mine calls this our wiring. I think that's the perfect term.

Wiring develops out of that mysterious blend of nature, nurture, culture, and early life experience. It is the way we're made, designed, and it is through this wiring that we engage the world. While many things can repress, impact, or expand our basic circuitry, as long as we're alive it can never be destroyed.

Wiring contributes not only to who we are as individuals, but also to what we seek and find outside ourselves. No two people see or experience the world the same way. There are certainly broad similarities, which lend lasting popularity to systems of classification like astrology and the enneagram, yet ultimately there are as many worlds as there are people. None of us has the capacity, no matter how hard we try, to live someone else's life.

In an age of staggering scientific achievement, it's easy to cling to the idea of objective truth, of a real world existing "out there" beyond our perception. Real or not, this land of physical laws and uniform processes is never how we experience life "in here." The history of science, from its inception to the present day, has been rife with clashing egos. In addition, how we interpret scientific data has wiring written all over it.

Recently, for example, researchers discovered a region of the brain that seems to house the religious impulse. For nonbelievers this suggests that God is just another biological need. For believers it indicates the portal through which divinity enters. Personality, in the end, is a vital aspect of science *and* nature. Attempting to escape it, no matter how "objective" our approach, is another way to deny what is.

All of this is not to say that we're locked into one single circuit. Instead, understanding the role of personality helps us to live the questions. Living the questions, in turn, allows us to distinguish between what is fluid and fixed.

In the case of my own personality, I have a tendency toward the analytical. Those who know me might consider that a massive understatement. With no effort on my part whatsoever, my mind loves to seek out causes and patterns. It's a key element of my wiring. It's been there since I was young and will remain till I die. To resist it, or attempt to rewire it, would lead to certain failure.

It's also true, on the other hand, that I often employ analysis as a defense. I hide in my head. A great asset becomes a severe liability, and the result usually looks something like this:

> *Where does he get off, criticizing me like that? He's just a colleague, for godsake. I think he's so insecure that putting me down makes him feel better. Yeah, that must be it. And he cut me off before I was even finished. What's that about? Y'know I bet he has Attention Deficit Disorder. Would he listen to me if I suggested it? Probably not. He doesn't listen to anyone but his wife. Should I mention it to her? No way. Talk about a blind spot — she worships the ground he walks on.*

If I remain unaware of what's happening, such a spin-out can last minutes, in some cases even hours. When aided by the power of presence, however, I'm able to catch myself early on.

What is happening right now?

Thinking. Lots of it. I'm trying to get a fix on my colleague. I'm trying to figure out all his negativity.

What is happening right now?

I'm resisting how much his criticism got to me. Covering up how much it really hurts.

Can I be with it?

Now that I'm aware it's there...yeah.

What's fixed, in this example, is a penchant for analysis. What's fluid is my defensive posture. That posture is a type of contraction. It dams the flow of energy inside my wiring. It keeps me unnecessarily stuck.

Over the years, feeling a little one dimensional, I sought to balance out my intellect with sports. I loved to play and was always pretty good. This was a natural choice. It was in harmony with my wiring. By contrast, during college, I once tried to fix my own car. The idea of being mechanical appealed to me, even though I consistently tested low for that aptitude. I spent one entire Sunday trying to replace a faulty part. In the end I failed. I got some help from my roommate. He did the whole job in exactly five minutes.

If I really wanted to be a mechanic, no one would have stood in my way. But it wasn't in my makeup, and life is short, so from then on I got my car serviced.

On the surface this may seem an obvious point. Yet how many of us, resisting the way we're wired, spend years trying to match someone's ill-fitting standards? Or, sadder yet, how many of us set those standards ourselves?

For instance:

What is happening right now?

> I'm studying for finals. Or at least trying to. I can't seem to focus at all. How am I ever going to make it through med school if I'm always so scattered?

Can I be with it?

> Why should I? No one else in my family is like this. It all came easy so for them. They were born to be doctors.

What is happening right now?

> I'm resisting the fact that this is hard for me.

> I'm resisting the fact that I don't like it, that I don't really want to stay.

Can I be with it?

> With dropping out? They would die. I think I
> would die. I mean what else would I possibly do?

The issue here isn't whether or not to stay in med school. It's about owning the resistance, about letting go of a false self-image. Only when that happens, whether as a doctor or anything else, will our subject be able to expand completely and make clear decisions.

Denying who we are leads to serious contraction. Striving to be who we are not does the same. In each case, if left to fester, these contractions will cast ominous shadows. If witnessed, however, and accepted, they have no other choice but to open.

Sometimes, when such dense contractions dissolve, they reveal vast, untapped parts of our being. Often the wires were severed early in childhood, or later by a traumatic life event. Resplicing them connects us with a seeming stranger, a part of us that we don't really know. This process can be enthralling. We may find brand new passions and talents. Yet, if we're not careful, it can also wreak total havoc.

One woman I know, after many years as a high-powered executive, encountered a long-repressed streak of rebellion. The power of this disowned trait was so overwhelming that it led her to abandon both work and family. She began acting like a wayward teenager, hanging out in bars and saying "No!" to anything remotely adult. Instead of accepting this streak and letting it merge with the rest of her, this woman acted out its every whim. She lost awareness, clung to a shadow, and contracted against everything else. It took many years, and tremendous pain, for her to restore a healthy balance.

Discovering all we are, and all we aren't, is the inevitable outcome of presence. Presence allows us to reclaim denied selves with awareness and discard false selves with ease. It also frees us from the misconception that "awakening" looks any particular way. Some of us are prone to anger. Some of us can't sit still. Some love to dance all night while others prefer a really good book.

Experiencing the difference between wiring and contraction allows us to stop searching for *the* way and begin living *our* way. We grasp that all people are wired, whether they like it or not. We learn to let them be, to value diversity instead of uniformity. And that, after so much resistance, feels positively electric.

CHAPTER 21

Swinging

The amount of presence we bring to thought
determines whether we become lost within it.

PAYING ATTENTION TO PERSONAL-
ity, we find that it's a self-perpetuating process. This causes us to
wonder what else, thought previously to be the product of effort,
might also operate on its own power. In short order, we arrive at
the realm of the mind.

For the purpose of our discussion, let's define the mind as the
part of consciousness that thinks, feels, desires, and senses. Let's
stipulate, along with recent scientific findings, that the mind is a
nonlocalized entity. Much of it resides in the brain, but it also
occurs throughout the body. Studying it from the outside we might
take momentary snapshots, or construct maps of its action, but
its ever-shifting nature is something which can never be repro-
duced or pinned down.

Thought, emotion, desire, sensation — over the next four chapters
we will look at these functions one at a time. Let's begin our exploration with thought.

THINKING ABOUT THINKING

Through presence, we're able to experience thought at work. We recognize that primarily it is a tool of investigation, indispensable in many circumstances but problematic in others. Thought probes, compares, reviews, and evaluates. It does this all day long, whether we want it to or not. It even continues at night, in the world of our dreams. Anyone who has attempted even a minute of meditation will testify that stopping thought is utterly impossible. At best, by enlisting our will, we can focus thought for periods of time.

If anything, thought is constantly restless. It is like a skittish primate, swinging through a thicket of trees. *Monkey mind* is the apt term used in Zen. When it comes to living the questions, thought is a resistance machine. It fills every pause with chatter. It swings us right out of the moment.

Thought loves to dwell in the past, reliving previous experience from every possible angle. It celebrates, regrets, muses. It lives to critique, looking for things that turned out badly and people who did us wrong. Above all it seeks to understand, fully, as if piecing everything together in just the right fashion will lay it all to rest. But the moment such a vision comes into focus, thought cannot abide. It finds more pieces, or whole new puzzles, since it's lost without a reason to churn.

The future, too, is a place where thought runs wild. It imagines, plans, plays out possible scenarios. It locates a desire in the present and then extrapolates its fulfillment in the future. No matter that the eventuality rarely turns out as expected. No matter that when it arrives, thought is already off on another trip.

Backwards and forwards, past and future. Thoughts carom chaotically between seconds, minutes, days, and years. And when for brief periods thinking lands in the present, it's usually with an eye for what's *not* there, what's amiss, what's in need of immediate change.

> *I'm cold. When's dinner? Why's he talking so much? Who's that? My back hurts. Should I smile? Should I leave? Everyone's ignoring me.*

The interminable chatter of thought has no sense of propriety. It functions at work, during sex, and in the middle of conversation or prayer. It serves a crucial role in our lives, but vastly overestimates its importance. Thought is like a steering wheel that assumes it's the engine, the chassis, the tires, and even the driver. None of this is a problem, or needs to be transcended, it's just one more part of what is. Accepting it, like we accept the prism of personality, allows us to be ever more present.

THOUGHT AND BLISS

The thinking mind is the part of you that is reading this book. It is also the part that mulls over the stories and ideas here, weighing their validity and importance. But the thinking mind is never the part that experiences bliss. That's neither its role nor its capacity. In fact, thought can't even relate to bliss. The two are like oil and water.

Previously, we've seen how thoughts can agitate the stillness necessary for living the questions. In this way they impede our presence, limit our access to bliss. But thought can also work from the opposite direction, stealing us from the bliss we find. The varieties of this theft are infinite, but here's a representative example.

What is happening right now?

> I'm feeling expanded, connected. Not ecstatic, just a quiet, peaceful joy. Asking the questions like this opens me even further.

Can I be with it?

> Mmm-hmmmm. Forever. That headache I had before is gone. I wonder what caused it? Maybe I should stop drinking coffee. But I love coffee! I don't want to give it up! What good is staying healthy if I can't even enjoy my life?!

From bliss to blech. In seconds flat. Courtesy of just a few stray thoughts. It's natural, whenever this happens, to curse ourselves and bear down harder. We vow that next time we'll remain strong, snag-proof, only to repeat the pattern all over. But this, like everything else, needs to be fully accepted. To pursue bliss and eschew thought is nothing short of resistance. It's a trap, and the only way out is to gain awareness and then live the questions.

While bliss and thought never work together, they do function simultaneously. This often leads to comic juxtaposition. I've been suffused by the most awesome bliss imaginable and found myself, at the exact same moment, planning what to have for lunch. Or debating which movie to see. Or wondering if it's time to clip my nails.

This dual arising is not only common but inevitable. Not even the greatest monks and meditators are immune. Thoughts constantly arise in their minds because that's what thoughts always do. Knowing this becomes quite a relief. It leaves one less way we can fail.

On the other hand, it is certainly possible for thoughts to slow down, spread out, and diminish in force and volume. Yet we can't will it, or push it, or try in any way whatsoever. This only transpires — no surprise — through the consistent practice of presence. The more we accept, the more we expand. The more we expand, the more bliss is free to flow. Increased bliss is like a cresting river. It washes thought to the banks of our awareness. Sometimes, at flood stage, we can hardly even tell it's there.

RACKING MY BRAIN

But what relevance does this have for everyday life? Don't most of us bear responsibilities, both personal and professional, that require us to be immersed in thought? And if thought and bliss don't intersect, doesn't that place bliss out of reach? Luckily, no. The amount of presence we bring to thought determines whether we become lost within it.

As I mentioned in the last chapter, I'm a cerebral guy. A big thinker. So this arena has fascinated me, challenged me, and shown me my own limitations. When I started paying attention to the way I think, the first thing I noted was a tendency to lose awareness of my body. It was as if, for long stretches of time, nothing but thought existed. I would return from these mental excursions in a fog, depleted, having robbed my body of its essential energy.

The second thing I noted, while witnessing my method of thought, is that sometimes it became a form of contraction. I found that to "rack my brain," as the saying goes, required an energetic scrunching up. I became tense and frustrated during those moments, and mental breakthroughs rarely arrived. But sometimes when I gave up, and then set about a distracting task, the breakthrough would suddenly occur.

This led me to understand, from the inside out, that I don't manufacture my thoughts at all. Even when I make a huge show of effort, of concentration, thoughts come of their own accord. My only actual job is to create a conducive internal environment. Leaving my body, or contracting it rigidly, is anything but thought-friendly.

Armed with this new understanding, I've begun exploring ways to think and expand at once. One thing that helps is to think "through my feet." This simple technique involves consciously rooting a piece of my awareness to the ground as each train of thought leaves the station.

But the best tool I've found is a vibrating beeper, set to go off every few minutes, which calls attention to any disconnected thinking and gently buzzes me back to the now. I use the beeper from time to time, like a refresher course, especially during intense, mental effort. Though the practice may seem a tad Orwellian, in fact it's a great delight. With the aid of the beeper I have learned that my *productive* thought usually comes in very short spurts, and that it is never impeded by presence.

The opposite is true, of course, since presence increases expansion. In an expanded state, thought and bliss flow closely together. Their alignment and proximity allow me to shift freely from one to the other. I get more thinking done than ever before and feel nourished instead of fatigued.

Since each of us is wired uniquely, your own experience may differ. I encourage you to experiment with thought, play with it, and witness what happens when you give it some room. Perhaps you'll discover, through all that thinking, that bliss remains right nearby.

CHAPTER 22

Swirling

Trapped emotion, by far, is the most common type of contraction. Releasing that emotion, whether ancient or current, restores us to the present tense.

IF THOUGHT SWINGS, EMOTION tion swirls. It pours through us from a mysterious spring, sometimes in great gushes, other times in meandering streams. It moves according to its own rhythm, but it always moves. Along the way, emotion asks for only one thing — acceptance. Acceptance is the wind which draws the current along.

The experience of raw emotion is exhilarating. It's what lets us know we're alive. This is true of emotions both pleasing and painful. When we're expanded, there's even an alluring aspect to envy, anger, and grief. But often, when contraction impedes the flow, the last thing we want to do is feel.

When we contract against the flow of emotion, it is usually because we're afraid. We don't trust that our negative feelings will ever change, or fear that they'll destroy us in the process. But as with all contraction, this turns out to be a no-win approach. The unwanted emotion just sticks around, trapped by the dam of our resistance, growing turbulent and projecting like mad.

Previously, I've described my biggest past contraction — disowned vulnerability. At a very young age I made an unconscious decision not to feel the hurt and isolation that were part of my upbringing. It was a protective device, and not such a bad one. I simply pretended that none of that existed, that I was free and resilient and strong. Later though, it became urgent that I accept the opposite.

For me, accepting all that pain required a safe space and a skilled therapist. At first it felt cataclysmic, like walking into a hurricane. For months on end I was wary, fragile, a functioning open wound. But then, when the contraction yielded more fully, something surprising happened. For the first time in my life it felt good to feel bad. I experienced the solace of free-flowing emotion, that paradoxical sweetness of just letting feelings be.

Since then, many of my early wounds have healed. And now, after I learned to welcome all emotion, acceptance occurs much more swiftly. If I recognize a contraction in the moment and am able to live the questions, any dammed emotions are freed to flow. Usually, if nothing major is happening, they are soon subsumed by bliss. If not, I consider that an important sign. Somewhere denial is hiding. It's time for a serious search.

Such searching can reveal emotional contractions so powerful that they shape our lives. A Latino scholar, not far from my hometown, provides a helpful illustration. Though respected and successful, he suffered often in his career from academic racism. Over the years he came to take it for granted that people would underestimate or demean him. This gnawed at him and caused him to bristle defensively at the slightest provocation. Eventually he began *looking* for a fight, for one more chance to prove his detractors wrong.

But then he had a heart attack, and during his convalescence he began to see things differently. He realized that though the pain of encountering prejudice was inevitable, his internal reaction to it wasn't predetermined at all. After its initial sting, he was free to clamp down in dogged resistance, or to accept the bigotry and expand in spite of it. Once he was fully recovered and returned to his university, he had an immediate opportunity to test this out.

A visiting foreign dignitary, probably without even knowing it, made a racially offensive remark. The scholar contracted instantly. He felt a seething rage in his belly. His head pounded and his fists clenched. He imagined an op-ed piece, a press conference, a possible campus protest. But then he caught himself and became aware of his old pattern. Although he didn't use the language of this book, his process was the same. In our terms, what he recounted for me later went something like this:

What is happening right now?

> I'm resisting this man's ignorance. I'm wanting to lash out against him so I won't have to feel the pain he's caused.

Can I be with it?

With his ignorance? I guess so. With the pain? I
want to, but… Fighting against it is so ingrained.
Almost like a reflex.

What is happening right now?

I'm getting it. I'm opening back up. I see how all
that resistance is just punishing myself. How it
hurts me more than he ever could.

There's nothing wrong, of course, with op-ed pieces, press
conferences, and protests. In some cases they might be the best
choice. This time, however, the scholar found an appropriate
moment to take the dignitary aside and have a quiet conversation. The dignitary heard him out, apologized, and thanked him
profusely for handling the situation so thoughtfully. Through
presence and the clarity it brings, the scholar found a decisive,
effective, expanded course of action.

Though most of us don't encounter persistent oppression,
our lives are filled with innumerable events like the one above.
Intentionally or not, our parents, siblings, lovers, friends, and
acquaintances often hurt us with their words and deeds. Furthermore, the normal flow of everyday life often teems with irritation
and annoyance. Our resistance to such events can grow and fester, or instead we can stay present and open. There is never a
right or wrong decision, but it is our own happiness, our own
bliss which hangs in the balance.

OBSESSION

Besides the standard contraction, there's a second way we obstruct emotion. It is related to the *analyzing* described in chapter 12 and the *wallowing* from chapter 19. An experience occurs that is so traumatic, so unacceptable, it deluges us with emotional pain. We become entranced, obsessed. We probe the pain, inspect it, cling to it for dear life. The signature feature of this obsession is a desire to have it all make sense. Underneath that desire is a hidden hope. If we ever understand completely, the problem might go away.

The demise of a precious relationship, the death of a loved one, the onset of a serious illness — all these shocks can send us into an obsessive tailspin. If the pain momentarily subsides, we become disoriented. We stir it, poke it, until it reaches full force once more. Most of us have a memory of watching someone in the throes of such obsession, of wondering what we might say to set them free. From the outside, it's clear how much the cycle is self-perpetuated. On the inside, however, there is little awareness whatsoever.

Many people respond this way to much smaller events. They consider themselves passionate, deeply emotional, and even wear it as a badge of pride. But the truth is they're *avoiding* emotion. Instead of sinking directly into the pain, they smother it with endless fixation. What looks like surrender is disguised contraction. Obsessing about emotion is another way not to feel it.

The relationship between thought and emotion is intricate

and reciprocal. Paying close attention, we find that in everyday life one seamlessly triggers the other. When contraction is involved, however, this triggering locks into a feedback loop. Since nothing can move, it all just gets louder and louder. Sensing such a loop is a shortcut to awareness.

What is happening right now?

> I can't believe they fired me. I was the hardest working person at that company. There has to be more to it. A rumor? A resentment? I need to know!

What is happening right now?

> Here I go again. Asking the same questions I've asked for weeks. Churning it up to keep from breaking down.

Can I be with it?

> I'm afraid. I might not be strong enough. Deep breath. Two or three more. Okay. Maybe I'm finally ready.

If our thoughts are drawn to the same subject over and over, as seen above, it's a good bet they hide trapped emotion. Conversely, if a painful emotion overstays its welcome, more than likely we're stuck obsessing. As in:

What is happening right now?

> I'm depressed. What else is new? Ever since I lost my job, it's the same thing every day.

Can I be with it?

> I am being with it! It's all I ever think about!

What is happening right now?

> Oh, I get it. I need to *stop* thinking about it. I need to let go and let it all move.

A similar relationship exists between emotion and compulsion. If difficult or destructive patterns keep appearing in our lives, usually that signals emotional contraction. Likewise, if we harbor serious emotional contraction, those patterns are almost bound to appear.

That is not to say that once we locate and release those contractions, life will magically go our way. It might or might not. What will change, for certain, is how we respond to whatever it brings. Freedom from contraction gives us choice and space. Where before were just knee-jerk reactions, now possibility abounds.

THE WAY WE FEEL

Looking at feelings this way leads to an obvious question: How can we tell the difference between a trapped emotion and one that is merely slow-moving? In other words, when are we getting over something at our own pace versus harmfully holding on? In my experience, presence always provides the answer. Obsessive emotion has a clenched quality. It's like trying to breathe and hold one's breath at once. Genuine emotion, on the other hand, actually encourages expansion. It's *un*clenching. No matter how grim, and no matter how lengthy, it never fails to open us up.

Trapped emotion, by far, is the most common type of contraction. Releasing that emotion, whether ancient or current, restores all of us to the present tense. But that's where our commonality ends. The way we feel and how much we feel stem mostly from our personal wiring. While it's easy to label people too stoic, or over-emotional, often that's just the way they're made. Similarly, what we do with our emotions is wiring-based. An extrovert may yell at the drop of a hat and weep at the slightest pain. An introvert, by contrast, may experience the exact same depth of feeling without displaying a single sign.

None of us, of course, is strictly one or the other. We are each wired uniquely and with awesome complexity. Rafting our emotional rapids allows us to find out who we are and how we work. Racing for shore, though common, is like fleeing from life itself.

CHAPTER 23

Twitching

Even if all our dreams came true, it would never be enough. The nature of desire is to constantly crave.

WHILE FEELING CALLS OUT for acceptance, impulse demands immediate action. All of our hungers — for sex, drugs, alcohol, money, power, approval — assault us relentlessly. Many of us spend our lives in blind obedience, pursuing a personal constellation of desire with little sense of choice or control. The force of these urges is so visceral, so hypnotic, that it often crushes any opposition from wiring, thought, or emotion.

Civilization and morality exist, in part, to regulate instinctive drives. They succeed to a degree. The human ability to delay gratification also plays a mediating role. In the end, however, we're still left with the *experience* of desire. Our lives, as a result, are a perpetual negotiation. We condemn our impulses, combat them, sublimate them, or selectively give in. The more it seems we have things in check, the greater the chance of springing a leak.

To compound the issue, many of our impulses are in direct conflict with one another. We need risk *and* security. We covet food *and* fitness. We long for monogamy *and* variety. Some days, our inner world feels like nothing but a gruesome battleground. Our sense of cohesion is the first casualty.

Eventually, for some of us, there comes a transformative moment. The insatiable quality of desire makes itself painfully clear. We realize that even if all our dreams came true, it would never be enough. New ones would instantly take their place. Just as the nature of thought is to continually churn, the nature of desire is to constantly crave.

The best example might be sex. Everyone knows the vice-grip that lust can exert and how difficult it is to deal with. The pursuit of sexual gratification can cause otherwise decent people to lie through their teeth and betray the ones they love. Religious leaders ignore their own teachings, and politicians gamble all their power. Much of this comes from the inability to tolerate lust itself. Just to be with it, for some, is worse than wrecking the rest of their lives.

And that's just to *get* sex, not about what happens during. No matter how much a partner excites us in the beginning, often the magnetism fades. Even if we never become unfaithful, our minds inevitably stray. We fantasize about everything that's not present — other people, other places, plus our own special blends of taboo. In the midst of indescribable pleasure, at the height of desire, often we're not even there.

There's nothing wrong, of course, with sexual fantasy. Thankfully, our preferences are a private matter. Yet the prevalence of fantasy speaks volumes about our inner enslavement.

We take for granted that sex with the same person grows routine, that it needs to be spiced up. We get off on what's *not* happening instead of showing up for what is. While sometimes fantasy grants a delightful change of pace, other times it's just good old resistance.

Recognizing the nature of desire allows us to watch it closely. We find that impulse, at its core, shelters a form of contraction. It identifies something that's lacking from the current moment and then contracts against that lack. The impulse, unsatisfied, cannot be endured. Reality is wrong. In this way, like thought, desire is a resistance machine.

There is no easy way to live the questions in the throes of desire. Still, it *is* possible. In lieu of twitching at every command, or taking refuge in cold showers, we can learn to bathe our desires with presence. Many desires, it turns out, flow through us just like emotion. At first they seem dense and entrenched. We've just got to have that coat, that car, that house. But then those same objects, with the passage of time and a dose of awareness, come to gradually lose their allure.

Other desires lead to deeper contractions, which turn out to be their actual source. This happened to a man on my basketball team. At a business convention, he met a client from across the country, flirted with her over drinks and dinner, and found himself on the brink of an extramarital affair. Then somehow he escaped to his hotel room and took a moment to collect himself.

As the adrenaline surged, he tried not to think about his

wife. But thoughts of her kept resurfacing. With each one he grew more and more angry. It turned out he had a whole laundry list of grievances against her. His dalliance, in large part, had been fueled by this latent conflict. Acknowledging it didn't dim his desire completely, but just enough to keep him out of trouble.

STATE OF EMERGENCY

Some desires, deeply innate, persist no matter what. Take the case of my neighbor, a graphic designer approaching forty. Like many single women of her age, she has a great desire to get married and start a family. With each year that passes her desire intensifies. At the same time, short of her goal, she grows increasingly frightened and tense.

She's also very resistant to introspection. When I showed her an early draft of this book, she agreed, reluctantly, to live the questions regarding her predicament. Here's an account of her first attempt.

What is happening right now?

> I'm frustrated. And angry. Everywhere I look there are happy families. Why don't I get to have one?

What is happening right now?

> I'm comparing myself to other people. I'm feeling

envy. I'm feeling victimized. My brow's furrowed
and I'm grinding my teeth. I'm resisting growing
old alone.

Can I be with it?

No! I refuse! This is not the life I was meant to
live! And what is this "be with it" anyway? There
are a million ways to "be" with something. What
the hell does that actually mean?!

Needless to say, my friend wasn't enjoying her experiment.
She felt threatened, like the questions were meant to deny her
desire. I explained that acceptance is an *internal* process, not a
sentence to solitary confinement, and that choosing it wouldn't
mean forfeiting her dream. She'd be even more free to pursue it, I
added, because the end result would bring her clarity, confidence,
and an abundance of positive energy. Finally, I told her that "being" with something is straightforward, simple. It means embracing the present moment as is, relating to it as a starting point
instead of a state of emergency.

Later, after her initial defensiveness subsided, she gave it another try.

What is happening right now?

I'm 38 years old and single. I live alone in a small
flat. I make a nice living and have great friends

but I'm not fulfilled. I really want to find a wonderful man, to get married and have a family. Yes-
terday.

Can I be with it?

With my life right now? As long as I can still want
it to be different...yes. With all the longing I have
inside? That's a lot harder.

What is happening right now?

I feel a bit lighter, relaxed. Like I'm under an ounce
less pressure.

A few weeks after our encounter, my friend called to tell me a
story. A woman in her building, with the same ticking clock, decided to give up all hope. Forsaking even the possibility of marriage, she set about just living her life. She signed up for exten-
sion classes and booked trips she had wanted to take forever. And
then a few months later, lo and behold, she walked smack into
the man of her dreams. Now she was getting married. It was almost like a fairy tale.

Upon first hearing the story, I was concerned that my friend
took away the wrong message from it. I thought she had decided
that bargaining was the way to go and that if she pretended not
to desire her desires, they would magically come true. But luckily
my friend had avoided that trap. She saw, instead, that this woman
had found a way to stop resisting and start *existing*. We both agreed

that in the kind of expansion that followed, almost anything is possible.

When the objects of our desire elude us, yet we can't let go, the present tense starves for attention. We can soon become empty, lifeless, as if strung out on a deadly drug. Living the questions, by contrast, is never a dour affair. The current moment remains full, vibrant, and ever-changing. We may indeed strive for the same goal and work for it with even more passion, yet we don't attach our well-being to the outcome.

The worst thing that can happen, to some of us, is actually achieving our goals. For a time it creates the illusion that lasting happiness is a result of success. It reinforces the treadmill and binds us tighter to our next objectives. Sexually speaking, that's exactly what happened to one of my college roommates. After a series of frustrating dating experiences during adolescence, he was filled with rage toward women. His mind swam with dark, negative fantasies.

Then, without even consciously trying, he met a string of women who wanted to live these fantasies out. While sweet and innocent on the surface, they all thrived on perverse role-play. At the time, he thought he'd died and gone to heaven. But with each new conquest, his needs grew more intense. His heart, simultaneously, was closing little by little.

Later, after years in a Twelve Step program, he lost all attachment to this cycle. His rage was finally healed, so those dark scenarios had no inner fuel. Looking back, he sees how the blunt edge of desire had denied him the heart's subtler graces. He was busy. He couldn't be bothered with bliss. And bliss, as we know, won't come when it isn't welcome.

THE PARADOX OF AWARENESS

Even when we're openhearted, finding worldly fulfillment can lead to great challenge. A wonderful relationship, for example, can imbue our lives with love. Yet it can also trick us into believing that our well-being *depends* upon our lover and that the end of the relationship would only bring doom. Likewise, the birth of a child can explode us into new territories of wonder and appreciation. But what about when tragedy strikes? If harm or even death came to that child, would it inevitably spell the end of our joy?

It doesn't have to, as long we continue to live the questions. Living the questions permits us to see all the places where desire impedes acceptance, where it links our presence to specific conditions. For me, in addition, it helps penetrate the seeming paradox of awareness.

Previously, I thought that detaching from experience meant becoming clinical and removed. I thought people who lived life to the fullest were those who parachuted out of planes and didn't take no for an answer and loved till they broke in pieces. Sitting on a meditation cushion, or doing nothing in *any* position, was a refuge for people who failed.

Somehow, though, I now find the opposite to be true. Only when we separate from our desires do we experience them completely. Only by experiencing them completely can we find our own path. This is also true of thought and emotion. Without witnessing it all there is no acceptance, and acceptance is what restores us to life.

CHAPTER 24

Stinging

*There's nothing like raw pain to blast
through all our plans and assumptions.*

TO LIVE LIFE AS WE KNOW IT
requires a body. There's no exception. Even people who claim
out-of-body experiences recount them from an embodied form.
Even when an altered state of consciousness takes us to a place of
pure spirit, our bodies don't disappear during the trip. If gods or
angels or other ethereal beings exist, we can only know them
through physical incarnation.

Having a body is what entitles us to sensation. Sensation includes not only the five external senses — seeing, smelling, touch-
ing, tasting, hearing — but also our internal perception. A gut
feeling, after all, presupposes the existence of a gut. Mythic lore
is filled with deities who long for the thrills of the flesh, who
consider sensation a great privilege. Sometimes we human beings agree.

Of all the things people desire, pleasurable sensation ranks
high on the list. A perfect meal, a great buzz, rousing speed, sump-
tuous sex — we love the ways they make us feel. Frequently these
pleasures blend with thought or emotion, while on occasion

they're a stand-alone rush. Either way, we crave them for their central gift — expansion.

BATTLING OUR BODIES

Not far into our pursuit of pleasure we encounter a disturbing fact. Bodies don't always cooperate. They expand and contract with a mysterious agenda all their own. During a prized vacation we're felled by a migraine. At the amusement park we pull a muscle. On the first day of our honeymoon, of all times, we get up on the wrong side of the bed.

Many of these misfortunes have an explainable cause, but just as many seem totally random. They're another reminder of how much of life we don't control. Who among us, for example, knows how to digest food? Oxygenate blood? Defeat an infection? For the most part these vital functions occur — just like thought, emotion, and desire — outside the realm of our will.

Contractions of the body, like all contractions, seek acceptance. Without it they're forced to go underground. That's often what allows a small complaint to develop into major disease. Even with acceptance, however, bodily contractions dissolve in their own good time. Yet staying present through the process provides many clues for renewed expansion. Three points deserve special mention.

The first point about physical contraction is that an enormous amount of our unhappiness comes from fighting with our bodies, or simply remaining ignorant of their influence. How many times, balled up with contraction, do we make bad decisions or lash out at loved ones? Sometimes just waiting awhile would make all the difference, yet it rarely happens.

Imagine two heads of state postponing a peace talk because one of them is in a bad mood. Or short of that, how about if the talks began with a simple acknowledgment of what's happening. "I'm a little irritable today. Let's make sure to factor that in." Sounds ridiculous, until we ponder the lives it might save.

The second point about physical contraction is how deeply it impacts thought and emotion. When we're in bed with the flu, for example, everything can look hopelessly bleak. Families, finances, work, and relationships are all nothing but misery. Even a precious partner fills us with disgust. Suddenly, uninvited, the mind prepares an entire laundry list of our partner's faults. *Loud, bossy, weak, dumb*. If we're able to disembark and watch the gloom train roaring past, the spectacle is often quite humorous.

The third point about physical contraction is a great relief. Even in the midst of it, we're still able to choose bliss. No illness, no injury, no inexplicable ache can ever keep us from living the questions. Living the questions allows us to identify and accept the condition of our bodies from moment to moment. In the expansion that results, there's room for an ailing body *and* bliss. Wherever there is space, even just a tiny crack, bliss can find it and fill the vacuum. That is not to say it's easy, or anything close to automatic. In fact, in the presence of great pain, sometimes it seems downright impossible.

THE POWER OF PAIN

There is nothing like raw pain to blast through all our plans
and assumptions. There is nothing like raw pain to show us a
clear picture of ourselves. Pain slams us into the here and now
with the power of its sensation. Our usual escape hatches are
abruptly blocked. But what a price to pay for presence. All we
want is to get the hell out.

Of the many physical maladies in my own life, the most painful is a spastic colon. Periodically, and without warning, my di-
gestive tract goes into a blinding spasm. It can last anywhere
from ten minutes to an hour. Nothing speeds it up, and nothing
dulls the assault. Waiting it out is the only choice. This is relatively manageable at home but quite an ordeal on airplanes or in
meetings.

Every time it happens, I get a snapshot of my ingrained resistance. I know by now that it's best to lie down, so I usually do.
But then my mind begins to rehash the last few days. Over and
over it searches for a probable cause, even though I've never yet
found one.

What is happening right now?

Pain…pain…pain.

Can I be with it?

Sure. Whatever. Y'know I bet it was that Chinese
food. Or the string of late nights. But no, those

were both last week.

So — what else? Yoga class? The new prescription?

Next, ignoring the fact that nothing has ever helped, my mind reviews all treatment options.

What is happening right now?

Pain…pain…pain.

Can I be with it?

Of course I can. But should I try some aspirin? A hot bath? That new homeopathic remedy?

Finally, it's onto doomsday scenarios.

What is happening right now?

Pain…pain…pain.

Can I be with it?

For awhile, yes. But what if this time it doesn't subside? What if I have to live this way the rest of my life?

All right — that's enough. Screw expansion. Screw

bliss. Get me some morphine now!

Eventually, my mind rolls over.

What is happening right now?

Pain. Excruciating pain. But it isn't really constant.

It's ebbing a little now. Wait — here it comes again.

This time it's moving around a little. And I'm noticing how it shifts, subtly, like it's empty and then suddenly dense.

Can I be with it?

Well… I'll give it my best shot.

There's an odd comfort in feeling every bit of the pain, in showing up for the worst of it. Plus, no matter how horrible the sting, I only have to feel it one moment at a time.

When I open to the pain fully, when I breathe right through it, bliss does arrive. I choose it, lose it, choose it and then lose it again. At that point, though, I can see clearly that it never goes anywhere. I'm the one, in the grip of bodily breakdown, who decides to turn my back.

Severe as it is, this periodic pain of mine pales in comparison to other conditions. Some torments can ravage people beyond comprehension. Under such circumstances, it's tempting to say there's not even a smidgen of space for bliss. But in my experience that's not true. I know a woman, for instance, with extensive spinal and neurological degeneration. A few years ago her pain was flat-out intolerable, even with serious medication. Then she learned to be with it, to open all the way in its presence. The pain itself didn't change, but bliss graced her nevertheless. Now she lives with both and blesses the difference daily.

Every situation, of course, presents its own unique obstacles. Generalizations can't just whisk them away. In fact, there are certain times in our lives when it's not feasible to expand into pain. Our responsibilities require us to keep going, to repress the sensation, or numb it with drugs. Or, ironically, sometimes numbing the pain is precisely what permits us to remain present. If either of these things happen, *that's* what is happening. There is no reason to judge ourselves harshly. In addition, every once in awhile we're just not willing. It is not about good or bad, can or can't. We perk up at pain's screaming siren, think it over, and say "not right now."

It is helpful, however, to gain awareness of two common attitudes towards pain. One can be described as deeply stoic and prizes the ability to stand firm in pain's grip. This approach is like resistance on steroids. Everything seems fine for awhile, until the inevitable violent explosion.

The other attitude, though similar, wears a spiritual guise. Common in many ascetic sects, it actually encourages pain and creates pain-seekers, who consider physical suffering a valuable training ground. If we can accept extreme pain, the argument goes, then lesser varieties should be no trouble at all.

Though useful, this argument carries an inherent shadow. It can cause us to weigh our acceptance against others', to compete and compare, and to adopt artificial standards of holiness. Either: *Look over here. I win. I can sit in the full lotus for an hour.* Or: *My knees ache after only five minutes. I can't bear it. There must be something wrong with me.*

PHYSICAL EDUCATION

When we decide to just be there, minus any strategy whatsoever, pain can then surrender its secrets. Much pain is past emotional contraction that has lodged in the body. This type of pain feels immovable at first, then yields with consistent awareness. Other pain, totally current, sends a very direct signal. Usually it's a stop sign — stop sitting, stop eating, stop working. These signals urge us toward immediate and simple solutions. Following their lead can avert serious harm.

Over time, we sense the subtle distinctions between pain which calls us to action and pain which needs nothing but presence. If we're not careful, however, we fall into the interpretation trap. We leap right past acceptance in search of meaning. We look frantically for reasons, ascribe each symptom its own message. One healing system, popular in the 80s, actually linked every affliction to a spiritual lesson. There's nothing like the interpretation trap to yank us out of the moment. Compulsive deduction, as we examined earlier, make us reporters rather than active participants.

Compulsive deduction feels nothing like living the questions. Answers that arise without effort, that clarify with acceptance, have an inherent rightness about them. We don't figure them out as much as expand into them. What reveals itself is always intuitive and deeply personal.

In the center of my back is a small knot. Throughout my childhood no one ever noticed it. I only noticed it myself, as a college student, when I began training in modern dance. An orthopedic surgeon told me that three vertebrae were congenitally fused. A chiropractor disputed that and set to work trying to realign me. The knot didn't change much, but suddenly that whole area of my body came to life. I felt the need to stretch it constantly, and a vibrant feeling of electricity poured through me.

Later, in psychotherapy, I explored the area for emotional contraction. It was no accident, I came to see, that the vertebrae had closed in the area surrounding my heart. The more attention I paid to the area, the more it revealed to me. Sometimes the revelation came in great, mysterious releases of grief. Other times images and memories appeared. Throughout, needing not a shred of proof, I knew this to be a deep healing. In fits and starts, both physically and emotionally, the healing has continued ever since.

The stories of our lives are written in the body. The meanings of these stories belong to us. Living the questions is like sitting around an internal campfire, surrendering to the storyteller and relishing every twist and turn.

The body is a teacher, too, and sometimes physical suffering provides invaluable education. For a decade, I've lived with an illness known as CFIDS, or Chronic Fatigue Immune Dysfunction Syndrome. CFIDS saps a person's life energy. Whatever energy still exists gets apportioned in tiny doses, and there's rarely any warning before it's all used up.

Talk about a lesson in presence. We CFIDS people must be ever-attentive, ready to drop what we're doing in an instant. Likewise, we learn to seize liveliness whenever it arises. Some days I begin writing this book at noon, while other days it's impossible till ten at night. If fortune smiles, a workday might last six hours, but most often I'm limited to three or four. And one day a week, without fail, there isn't will for a single word.

Living with CFIDS has thrust me into a world of sleep, supplements, "miracle cures," and medical abstracts. Above all, though, it drowns me in my own resistance. I pine for the life I used to have, full of multiple projects and impressive vigor. Every once in awhile I pretend it's still here. I overexert and suffer a serious setback. What is just isn't good enough, until I remember to live the questions. Then, surrendering, I recall all that presence has taught me. I become a guy with a spastic colon, a bum back, a chronic illness, and a bliss that soothes every ache.

For some, sadly, resistance is a lifelong endeavor. No amount of pain or suffering can make even a dent in their armor. In the clutches of death, they may taste the sweetness of surrender for the very first time. The end of life may become its real beginning. Many of us have witnessed this first hand, at the bedside of someone we love. I'll never forget the face of my mother, ravaged with cancer, yet somehow more present, more peaceful than she had ever been. What a gift to share those final moments with her and to feel her newly opened heart. And how tragic it would have been, poetry aside, if she had kept raging against that good night.

CHAPTER 25

Stuck

It's only natural, while reading a book about bliss, to want some of the good stuff right now.

THERE IS A WAY IN WHICH TALK-ing about bliss can cheapen it. Too many words and bliss can become, alternately, pie-in-the-sky or downright prosaic. It can seem abstract, irrelevant, unrelated to the grit of our everyday lives. What's worse, descriptions of bliss can seem like a foreign language, like nails on a chalkboard to someone racked by pain and suffering.

Bliss, as we defined it, is nothing more or less than persistent joy and love in the absence of a cause. But what about when lots of causes are present for its opposite? What about when the slings and arrows of outrageous fortune have all managed to pierce one's heart?

At times like these we feel like screaming "You just don't un-derstand! No one can! I've tried everything but nothing helps!" Many roads lead to this quicksand. *Too fat, too poor, too sick, too sad.* No matter what gets us here, we end up stuck in the exact same way.

All these travails share one crucial aspect. They relate to the

conditions of existence. Our claim, whenever sinking, is that bliss
is impossible under the current circumstance. For those of you
who feel that way, who cling to life by a fragile thread, I'd like to
pose the following question.

Imagine that the conditions of your life remained the same,
yet somehow bliss was in your reach. Would you grab it? Think
about what this means. You might be a blissful three hundred
pounds, or blissfully bankrupt, or blissfully betrayed. In other
words, would you accept a bliss that left your situation improved
in no way whatsoever?

For many people, the answer is no. To them such a bliss seems
useless, almost like a slap in the face. If you're one of those people,
please be aware of that choice. Please be aware that it's *your* choice.
The bliss which you deny is free and eternal, yet it does require
your acceptance. There's no penalty for turning it down, but it
costs nothing to give it a chance. Giving it a chance means that
you're willing to have a different experience. It doesn't guarantee
that experience, or offer a schedule for its arrival. Instead, it simply allows for the possibility.

I have a friend who's suffered with a weight problem all her
life. As anyone in that situation knows, the weight is just the tip
of the iceberg. My friend spins out often into a cycle of shame,
rage, fear, and anxiety. Sometimes, and this is no exaggeration,
she would rather be dead than fat. Bliss, certainly, would make
her life an oxymoron.

Lately, however, my friend has begun to live the questions.
The answers she finds are often deeply disturbing.

What is happening right now?

> I feel stuck. Trapped in my body. Like I can't really be myself or do any of the things I want.

But why?

> Because…well…fat people don't have a right to. They get in the way, take up too much space.

Is that true, or is it just my own belief?

> Both. It's the way society treats us. And over time we come to internalize it.

But is it a fact? Is it what's really happening?

> Inside of me, deep down — yes. *I* believe it's the truth.

Can I be with it?

> I don't know! My God! I'm horrified that I do that to myself!

What is happening right now?

> I'm trembling, crying. I don't want to have that belief! I want it out of me!

Can I be with it?

> Not right now. I'm too ashamed. This one's going to take some time.

More and more, my friend is taking that time. She permits herself to feel all the shame, all the pain, all the way. It helps her understand that in many respects she *chooses* to suffer. She sees that it *is* possible to be heavy and blissful. Increasingly, she expands into that very experience.

Another one of my friends is a harried mother. Her babies demand constant attention. The pressures of childrearing can lay waste to her patience. Often, even the simplest pleasures seem far from reach. In recent times, to top it off, she got very sick. Luckily, she chose to live the questions as part of her recovery. She gave herself the gift of presence and began to find bliss beneath all that stress.

Now, newly expanded, dealing with her kids has become much more gratifying. She describes the way that moment to moment acceptance creates a palpable shift in her energy. The kids can feel it right away, just as they can sense its absence. She's not perfect, and certainly wouldn't consider herself a role model, but every time a baby's wail signals resistance in the air, she quickly remembers what to ask.

CRADLING THE BABY

Even when we're willing to give bliss a chance, sometimes it still doesn't come. We ask and ask, accept and accept, and don't feel much of anything at all. When this happens, the first thing to do is review the *Art of Asking* (see chapter 12) and the ways our questions can house hidden resistance. Usually the chief culprit is forgetting our original intention. Bliss, remember, is the result but never the goal. Waiting around for bliss to show up just prevents the only way it can. Acceptance of everything, even of errant bliss, is what living the questions really means.

Suppose, then, that we're attempting to live the questions in earnest and not simultaneously subvert them. And suppose that expansion still seems to elude us. The present tense, in this case, is just a jumble of random stuff. Lots of contraction, lots of static, not much to recommend the process. It's possible, when this occurs, that we're still stuck on the second question. We're not sure what it really feels like to let things be.

Since modern culture thrives on assertion and is practically allergic to stillness, many of us share this block. We have the toughest time finding our way to non-doing. If this sounds familiar, read the next four paragraphs carefully. Read them a couple times. Then follow their instructions for about ten minutes before continuing. Hopefully, you will find yourself opening at least a little bit.

Lie down. Give yourself as long as it takes to get comfortable. Notice any tension throughout your body. Notice your mood, the quality of your thoughts. Just notice all that without trying to adjust it. Now let your focus diffuse. By that I mean don't look for anything in particular. If your mind seeks something to hold onto, just accept that. Don't study it or recoil from it or narrow your focus in any way.

This isn't a specialized meditation, so you don't need to employ a specific method. Just continue to relax your field of awareness. Each time something arises and your attention goes to it, accept it without getting entangled. If you do get entangled, as soon as you recognize it relax once again.

More than likely, you'll begin to evaluate your experience. *Am I doing this right? Am I forgetting something? Is it working? Should I quit?* Accept this questioning also, but don't worry about finding any answers. Let it exist in your relaxed awareness along with any sounds and sensations that appear.

If many things happen at once, keep widening your focus to include them. If nothing seems to happen, let nothing be what's happening. If contractions come, let them find their way without intervention. If bliss appears, so be it. When you're ready to end this exercise, take a mental snapshot of how you feel throughout your body and mind.

Living the questions, as touched upon in chapter 15, occurs at a level deeper than language. Perhaps you experienced it in the exercise. If your mind-body snapshot feels loose, fluid, then rest assured that expansion was encouraged. The more you return to that landscape, the more expansion you'll eventually find. I once heard a Buddhist nun compare this kind of awareness to a mother cradling her newborn. She's quiet, loving, attentive. As the baby squawks and fidgets and cries, the mother just smiles and rocks it gently.

GIVING THANKS

Even mothers, of course, often grow impatient. Likewise it's only natural, while reading a whole book about bliss, to want some of the good stuff right now. So if you're feeling stuck, or perhaps just need a little boost, consider this simple shortcut. The shortcut comes in the form of a word - gratitude.

William Blake, the great mystic poet, said "gratitude is heaven itself." Beholding what we're grateful for never fails to expand us, even when serious suffering is present. It melts away resistance and softens the edges of contraction. Sometimes, when we're stuck, people tell us to be grateful for what we have. This often feels like a rebuke and can immediately contract us further. But finding our own gratitude, in our own time, is one of the greatest gifts we can give ourselves. Better yet, if we can separate our gratitude from its causes, if we can actually become that heaven itself, the result is always akin to bliss.

In those rare moments that bitterness abounds, that you can't find a grateful bone in your body, even then the same breakthrough is possible. Just imagine, briefly, that death waits around the corner. Imagine that every last aspect of your life will disappear in no time at all. Think about the things you would miss most. These very things are what can fill you with gratitude. All you have to do is let them. And sometimes, when the pain is so bad you *want* it all to end, one grateful thought can puncture the dark.

The darkest hours for me occurred during the breakup of my marriage. At the time it was a horrific blow, the last thing I wanted, since by all accounts my wife and I had the kind of robust relationship which usually lasts a lifetime. I loved her and our partnership more than anything ever in my life. But now the whole thing was crashing around me, and I couldn't do a thing about it.

In the early days of our separation, my mind was a textbook example of obsession. Through every waking hour, I struggled to make sense of the mess. I analyzed, judged, bargained, and wallowed. Unwittingly, I fed my own pain by warring with it. Finally, when I gave up, when I accepted what was happening, so much just fell into focus.

The peace that came with acceptance helped me find the shadows in myself which had contributed to the current crisis. Suddenly, I could see my marriage with much greater clarity. I was still deeply wounded but also grateful for all the partnership had given me. That gratitude enabled me to live the questions, to accept all the pain like a prize. I remained open, shattered, and then one day bliss mended me whole.

PART FOUR

• • •

Beyond Bliss

CHAPTER 26

What a Dog Hears

*Opinions, beliefs, and values often
separate us from one another needlessly.*

GREAT SUFFERING ALMOST AL-
ways shatters us. We're left to pick up the pieces of our identity,
of all the assumptions we previously held. If we gather them together too quickly, though, a profound opportunity is lost. A shattered state grants us the chance to start fresh, to see ourselves
anew, to practice the most powerful form of acceptance.

But can we practice it in the absence of tragedy? Can we get
there without hitting bottom?

Living the questions, it turns out, is a great equalizer. It allows
every one of us, no matter the circumstance, to regenerate moment by moment. When we forego resistance and keep coaxing
ourselves gently to open, layer upon layer of armor reveals itself
and falls away. Think of it, if you will, as deliberate shattering.

WHO DO WE THINK WE ARE?

The armor that falls away involves our identity. It's about who
we've come to think we are. Early on, we learn to distinguish

ourselves by gender, race, religion, ethnicity, nationality, class, appearance, intelligence, and ability. *He's a smart, handsome, blue collar African-American Muslim with great mathematical aptitude.* Or: *She's a slow, plain, impoverished Mexican Catholic who excels at the violin.* In time, we add the whole gamut of wiring to our self-definitions. We see these things as defining our existence. We cling to them. Sometimes we even fight and die over them. Yet all of it's a function of fate, something that happens *to* us, something mostly out of our control.

The facts of our identity are another part of what is. To deny them is to live in resistance. To accept them, to be with them fully, permits us to see how they affect our lives. Immediately, we ascertain the vital distinction between identity and *identification*. While identity just is, identification requires our choosing.

Take nationality, for example. I'm an American. Unless I give up my citizenship that will always be the case. But how much does being an American inform my thoughts and actions? Some of it's automatic, unconscious even, but a great deal remains up to me. Do I identify with America in a patriotic way? Would I kill to protect its interests? Do I disparage people from other countries?

Identification with nationality, or any circumstance of fate, can lead to a powerful sense of belonging and community. But it can also lead to serious contraction. Identification with what we are often requires *dis*identification with what we're not. It can become an us versus them proposition, whether black vs. white, gay vs. straight, or man vs. woman.

Total presence, on the other hand, means accepting all these differences without clinging to them. It means if I ever find it necessary to oppose you — in politics, in court, wherever — I still accept you as I accept myself. In an expanded state, our hearts remain open and inclusive. We don't celebrate diversity because it's "right," but because it comes naturally. We don't love our enemies because Jesus said to, but because it's impossible to do otherwise.

US VS. THEM

A more subtle aspect of identity involves our opinions, beliefs, and values. While these aren't as fixed as factors of race, gender, and ethnicity, their roots stretch very deep. From the moment we can speak, we're encouraged to classify our likes and dislikes. *My favorite color is…My favorite food is…* At first these personal choices can shift with rapid succession and are easily manipulated by advertising and other influences. One day it's *Power Rangers*, the next it's *Transformers*. Then peer pressure exerts its iron grip. By high school, most of us end up in cliques that concretize and reinforce our affinities - jocks, stoners, nerds, etc. It takes a rare kid, in an even rarer environment, to cross those borders with any frequency.

The divisions within our alignments grow incredibly complex. Our clothes, hairstyles, music, speech, and habits all reflect them. Perhaps because it's not inherited, because to a large degree we create it, our taste takes on monumental importance. As a teenager, in love with movies, I found it almost impossible to stay friends with someone who didn't admire the same films as me. And if a certain picture offended me, and a friend of mine loved it, all hell would surely break loose. What began as a harmless exercise — *My favorite toy is… My favorite film is…* — became reason to write someone off.

Though my movie fascism may seem like adolescent ardor, all of us, as adults, organize our lives along the same lines. We pick as friends those we most relate to, join groups that reflect our views. We are constantly seeking surroundings that mirror our frame of reference. Whenever we grow and change, incorporating a new attitude, our affiliations shift accordingly.

None of this is a problem, of course, or anything to be resisted. It is simply an outgrowth of the way we're made. But paying attention to the power of perspective, just like all other aspects of mind, helps us uncover a bounty of contraction. We see how identification with our own perspective can create an endless stream of us vs. them. There's liberal vs. conservative, highbrow vs. lowbrow, city vs. country. Factionalism pervades all sectors of society, no matter how superficially benign. Battles rage between schools of yoga, methods of conservation, even types of charity. These battles are all predicated on the idea that there's a better way, a best way, a way that things should be.

HARD CHOICES

Sometimes life requires that we take sides, that we conclude for ourselves what is wise or foolish, good or bad, right or wrong.

But life never demands resistance. That is always *our* choice. Take abortion, for example, an issue which polarizes almost everyone and offers a profound challenge to staying open.

If you oppose abortion, the other side is comprised of murderers. If you support choice, the other side harbors bands of terrorists. No amount of negotiation, no amount of attempted compromise can ever bridge this fundamental gulf. So then how do we remain expanded in the face of it? How do we love our enemies when we view them as slaying the innocent and the righteous?

Acceptance, as always, is the answer. Of the myriad positions and attitudes involving this complex topic, none can stand in for the whole. Still, to underscore the way that living the questions is beneficial even in the most heated circumstances, let's look at one case from each side of the aisle.

First, suppose you favor the right to choose, and learn about the latest clinic bombing. It's bound to produce an immediate contraction. That first physical clenching, remember, is natural and unavoidable. But once you become aware of it, you can elect to live the questions.

What is happening right now?

> I'm feeling angry, and hurt, and frustrated that people would harm those providing a critical service.

Can I be with it?

I don't know. When I let it flow through me fully, I'm filled with visions of violent retribution. I'm afraid of what I might do.

What is happening right now?

I'm resisting my own rage. I don't want to feel like *them.*

Can I be with it?

Maybe. I can see, at least, where acceptance seems blocked within me.

Feeling like a killer, embracing the killer inside us, is nothing like actual killing. Truth is, we're all capable of every emotion, no matter how primal or seemingly uncivilized. Even the holiest sage might experience murderous fury. How we respond to such emotions is what makes the difference.

Whether we resist the clinic bomber within, or resist the clinic bomber without, resistance still rules the day. Accepting both, acknowledging their indisputable reality, is the only thing that can release our contraction and allow us to expand. From that point, no matter what action we choose, it will flow from our deepest truth.

Next, suppose you're protesting outside the local Planned Parenthood. The demonstration is legal and peaceful, yet inside you it's not peaceful at all. As dozens of pregnant women walk past, your stomach constricts and your face flushes. Difficult as it is, surrounded by other angry picketers, you live the questions right then and there.

What is happening right now?

> I'm mortified, outraged. How can people just disregard a precious human life?

Can I be with it?

> With my feelings, yes. And I can even be with the fact that abortion's legal. But I don't want to expand any further.

> I mean, why would I want to feel bliss in the face of such unspeakable cruelty?

What is happening right now?

> I'm choosing not to open all the way. I'm holding onto the feelings that constrict me.

Can I be with it?

> Look — I have to be mortified. I have to be outraged. Otherwise I just wouldn't be me.

In this instance, identification is hard at work. It seems to the protester that a certain amount of resistance is called for, actually *required* to sustain a sense of self. But our personalities, as we've seen, persist without any help whatsoever. And our emotions just freeze up whenever we try to sway their course.

There's nothing wrong with proclaiming a limit, with saying that under some circumstances we will only expand so far. Yet there's no price, either, for letting those limits go. The bliss that can result is nothing but the freest and fullest life force. It doesn't deny or diminish anything. In fact, it provides support, nurturing and courage for our most authentic convictions.

HOW IT IS

Living the questions has nothing to do with morality. It is neither a license to do anything nor an invitation to do nothing. In fact, it's amoral. It doesn't deny that life is full of tough decisions. It doesn't settle for fuzzy abstractions like "we should all love one another." Instead, it brings fresh awareness to the moral choices we all must make. It recognizes that many violent acts are committed in the blindness of contraction. It recognizes that expansion opens the heart, that love for ourselves and others leads to more satisfying results.

Still, no uniform set of values will work for everyone. Where, for instance, should killing stop? With babies unborn? With animals? With insects? With creatures our eyes can see? All of us, no matter how nonviolent, inflict some kind of killing in our daily routines. To contract against competing levels of purity can bring more violence into the world, not less.

From minor concerns like taste in film to major concerns like abortion, our perspective becomes the lens through which we see the world. Identification with perspective causes us to confuse what's right with what's right for us. Billions of us roam the world thinking we know exactly "how it is," yet most of the time we're in disagreement. Even when we find compatriots and link up with them, sooner or later our perspectives part company.

Bringing our perspectives into awareness and living the questions as they shade each moment, keeps us from being enslaved by them. Expanded, we're free to leave the lenses on, take them off, or develop new ones. In particular, we become wise to the ways that opinions, beliefs, and values often separate us from one another needlessly. We maintain our distinctive outlook, but at the same time widen our vision.

Whenever I get too contracted by my own perspective, I try to remember what a dog hears. A dog's perception of sound is far superior to that of humans. Its sense of smell is better, too. Other animals possess an amazing visual acuity or key in astoundingly to a certain group of stimuli. All living creatures share the same world, but we perceive it very differently. There is always so much more out there than what we're willing or able to find.

A dog's hearing humbles me. It encourages me to shatter my own armor. It makes me more curious and less sure. I become entranced with all I don't know rather than with what I do. I discover, in the end, how boring it is to live the answers.

CHAPTER 27

Hell

*The discrepancy between expectation and reality
becomes a snare that holds resistance in place.*

"HELL," IN THE FAMOUS WORDS
of Jean Paul Sartre, "is other people." It seems they never do what
we want and always get in our way. There's the woman with no
cash in the express line, or the man who keeps shouting in the
library. When we're late, someone's bound to drive a mile an hour.
When we're cruising, someone's bound to breathe down our neck.
Whether we stand firm and fight, or flee for the relief of solitude,
people stymie us at every turn.

The more important the goal, the more intense our frustration. Some of this frustration is just part of life, yet another thing
calling for acceptance. Much of it, however, is created by our
own resistance. In the same way that identification with perspective can reinforce contraction, so, too, can our expectations of
those around us.

EXPECTATION AT WORK

In every aspect of our lives, we carry a picture of the way people
should act. When they conform to our picture, we ride the tempo-

rary wave of expansion. When they fail us, we contract in rebound. In our careers, for example, we expect people to honor, appreciate, and promote us. If they don't, we feel like the world's off-kilter. The discrepancy between expectation and reality becomes a snare that holds resistance in place. No matter whom we blame — them, us, fate, God — expansion remains out of the question.

This happened to me for over a decade, as I pursued a career in screenwriting. With plenty of patience and determination, I struggled to make a living. I wrote script after script, fought for assignment after assignment. Over time, success began to come. I earned more and more money, qualified for better and better projects. Throughout, however, I never felt like I really "made it." I continued to see myself as an outsider, with my nose pressed against the glass.

As I began to live the questions and include my career in the field of awareness, it became clear to me what a powerful expectation I clung to. I saw how "making it" meant that everyone would finally love me. They would see how talented I was, how brilliant, and then anoint me as the next big thing. This dream of artistic approval was what *needed to happen*. Somehow, though, no one ever got the message.

Minus this bath of fame, and yearning for it so painfully, I experienced an ever-deepening disappointment. I contracted with bitterness against the entire entertainment industry. I saw it, not as a group of incredibly diverse individuals, but as a unified, punishing monolith. I felt that its refusal to recognize my genius was like a declaration of war. I was at war in my work, and became shell-shocked to the point of creative paralysis.

Letting go of my resistance and accepting all the pain trapped within it, I saw how neatly I had projected my personal story onto a totally impersonal business. Perhaps star status would come my way, or perhaps it never would, but no longer was it a prerequisite for my expansion. Finding the bliss of being, and learning how to choose it, freed me to unburden each new project from the weight of so much need. Ever since, the actual process of writing seems to glitter with its own rewards. From time to time the old story still takes hold, but with some gentle acknowledgment it quickly dissolves.

EXPECTATION AT HOME

Expectation leads to even greater contraction within our families. We develop a picture of the family we're *supposed* to have, and then judge our actual family against that standard. The standard used to be defined by television, but over the years we've all become wise to the cloying quality of most sitcom life. The Nelsons and Cleavers have given way to a more psychologically savvy ideal.

Now we want parents and siblings who love us unconditionally, support our endeavors, and empathize with all our problems. We want this regardless of whether we return the favor. And when our family members don't measure up, we contract against their every failure.

I have a friend who recently discovered this in her own fam-

ily. Her father is notoriously inattentive. When talking on the
phone during their weekly chats, he simultaneously watches TV,
fixes things, or carries on other conversations. The lack of her
father's undivided attention was driving my friend crazy. She'd
contract, complain to friends, judge him for his perceived rejec-
tion. Then she decided to live the questions.

What is happening right now?

> I just hung up with dad. As usual I feel small, hurt,
> roughed up and a little numb. There's a catch in
> my throat and a knot in both my shoulders.

Can I be with it?

> Well, a part of me says yes. But another part says
> no. It wants him to change, to grow up, to stop
> being a scattered little boy.

What is happening right now?

> I'm resisting the reality of who he is, what he's ca-
> pable of. Or…at least what I think he's capable of.

What is happening right now?

> I'm realizing that I have a whole set of beliefs about
> his limitations. Like — since he's always been this
> way, he'll always be this way.

What is happening right now?

I'm starting to see my own part in all this. And
not just my beliefs, but also my actions. I mean
I'm the one who always calls. I could stop calling,
or call less often.

Or what about discussing it with him directly,
without hostility? It's seems ridiculous to admit,
but I don't think I've ever really done that.

What is happening right now?

I'm thinking of that conversation and I'm afraid.
It's so volatile for me. I'm not sure I could pull it
off.

When our roles and patterns of communication are so entrenched, often it seems there's no other choice. My friend, suddenly, saw a whole range of choices. It was enlightening, but also
confusing. She was willing to let go of her expectation, yet un-
sure what she wanted to create in its place.

This kind of shaky nexus, between what is and what might
be, is another form of the fertile awareness we touched on earlier.
Though stressful, it's also vital. As long as we keep living the questions throughout, our truest answers always arrive.

My friend, ultimately, decided to embrace her fear. Once it
subsided a little, she confronted her father. Surprisingly, he claimed
utter ignorance of his inattention. Since she was reporting her
experience instead of attacking him, he felt free to accept her

accounting. He agreed to watch himself and to check in with her about it.

Over time, as it happened, he proved unable to change much. But my friend had changed remarkably. Their open dialogue had liberated most of her resistance. She saw that his fractured focus didn't mean he didn't love her, or that he wasn't a good father. She even found a way to joke about the problem whenever it occurred, to ask her father, with a smile in her voice, "What are you watching now?"

Expectation between parents and children works both ways. I know a mother who loves her grown son deeply but feels they should spend more time together. She's constantly urging him to come back home for visits and resenting him when he declines her requests. She has a specific notion of how many times a year they ought to see each other. It's about twice as much as his. She contracts furiously against the difference and often loses her temper, regardless of the fact that in all other ways he's an exemplary son.

What she has never contemplated, throughout their long-standing dispute, is that if he denied his own wishes and came home more just to please her, she'd be face to face with a son who *didn't want to be there*. Can such a situation ever truly satisfy? When our relatives do things unwillingly, out of guilt or obligation, who benefits? We nudge reality closer to our ideal but lose so much vitality in the process.

This dynamic plays out in countless families. People cling to an expectation of how their family members should be. Invariably, no one fits the bill. Resistance to what is creates years of resentment and rivalry. Acceptance, on the other hand, offers anyone the chance to opt out. The ensuing expansion is always sweet, even if nobody else goes along, and even if they contract further in response.

EXPECTATION IN LOVE

The expectation that occurs in families simply abounds in intimate relationships. We demand that our partners fit a check-list of criteria and then contract habitually when they don't.

He's too messy.	*She's too neat.*
He talks all the time.	*She's always quiet.*
He's overemotional.	*She's so repressed.*
He's not ambitious.	*She's downright greedy.*
He's sexually stale.	*She can't get enough.*

Neither gender nor sexual orientation makes a difference. We all do it to each other, all the time, no matter what quality earns the momentary spotlight. Accepting our partner's attributes may bring us closer or draw us farther apart. It may lead to change or more status quo. But it will always, results aside, increase the breathing room for both parties. And whenever we feel accepted, we're more available for productive dialogue.

I remember, with stunning clarity, the first time a girlfriend met me this way. Even though I wanted to be alone, I agreed to come over. I drove to her house with a chip on my shoulder. I expected her to resent my isolation, to call me "closed-off," and send me packing. So I tried to keep my feelings to myself, only she sensed them right away. With no other choice I came clean and prepared for the worst.

Instead she just listened, nodded, and then reflected back to me how bad I was feeling. She accepted my state, remained expanded, and affirmed me without an ounce of defensiveness. The reason I remember it so clearly is because nothing like that had ever happened to me. I had grown used to the idea that my feelings were wrong whenever they conflicted with someone else's. The possibility that I could just have them, that I could be myself no matter how closed-off, was truly revolutionary. I became so grateful, ironically, that I couldn't get enough togetherness. Such is the power of acceptance for everyone concerned.

EXPECTATION WITHIN

Of all the relationships we imprison with expectation, none holds a candle to what we do within. Our minds are filled with voices who find us lacking and take every opportunity to make it known. One moment we're too lazy, the next too manic. One moment we're too selfish, the next too spineless. And it's not just the "inner critic," which gets most of the press, but a whole host of competing entities all vying for their own agendas. They can sound like our parents, our enemies, and even our closest friends.

In fact they're all of the above, or facsimiles living inside us. Psychologists call them "introjects," and note the way they can outlive, and certainly outdo, the originals from which they sprung.

Introjects are like a virus of expectation, demanding that we be what we're not. We contract against their chorus of complaint and then resist its endless onslaught. But when we open to the cacophony, and give every voice a full hearing, something amazing often happens. They find, in the expansion, that there's room for all. They stop shouting. Once in awhile they even harmonize. Like everything else that's been resisted, they crave acceptance most of all. Sometimes, once they get it, they no longer care what we do.

Unfortunately, however, that's not always the case. Certain introjects are so strong, and so persistent, that they rule our lives with an iron fist. In chapter 25 I described a friend with a lifelong weight problem. In early adulthood that problem exploded into a full-fledged eating disorder. She became bulimic, prone to lots of dangerous purging. The key feature of her disorder was a terrifying inner tyrant, a paternal taskmaster who demanded thinness at the expense of all else.

For many years my friend couldn't find the awareness to hear this tyrant clearly. She followed every order with knee-jerk obedience. She not only thought the tyrant had her best interests at heart, but she thought its voice was her very own. She couldn't accept it because she was so identified with it. Its picture of how she should be just bowled over what she actually was.

PREFERENCE

Even now, as she lives the questions, my friend would rather be thin than fat. And that's to be accepted, too. But living the questions allows her, as well as the rest of us, to distinguish between expectation and preference.

Where expectation has a harsh, unforgiving quality, preference arises softly from our wiring and experience. When we find what we're looking for, we accept it without clinging tightly. When we encounter something that's not to our liking, we let it be and just say "no thanks." Expanded, we recognize that getting what we want won't save us, and not getting it won't destroy us. Right in the present, with things just the way they are, bliss is already here for the choosing.

While preferences acknowledge what exists, expectations focus on what doesn't. In place of acceptance we seek to overthrow reality, yet fail to note the flaw in that scheme. Things never turn out the way we imagine. Our expectations, realized, inevitably bring about new things to resist.

Personally, in regard to my movie career, I have no idea what greater success would be like. I may enjoy it more or prefer less pressure. Right now it's impossible to know. The same holds true for my friend with the inattentive father. If he were to pay her more complete attention, it might reveal a different, yet equally unappealing side of his character. And if that errant son spent more time with his mother, perhaps she'd start wishing he'd leave. My bulimic friend found this out firsthand. She purged herself lean, achieving the goal of a lifetime, only to discover that it made her brittle and edgy.

IMAGE

There's one final phenomenon, related to expectation and preference, which colors everything else explored in this chapter. It proves challenging even for the most expanded. It's the enormous amount of energy we spend trying to shape the way others see us.

Often, if we feel talented, we can't stand to be seen as mediocre. If we feel beautiful, we can't stand to be seen as plain. If we feel strong, we can't stand to be seen as weak. And if we're insecure about our talent, beauty or strength, it can feel even more crucial for others to affirm us. Either way, when they don't come through with that affirmation, major contraction is the inevitable result.

If none of this strikes a chord, watch yourself over the course of a few days. See how many times, in conversation, you choose your words carefully to come off a certain way. See how many times you gauge the assessments of your listeners, shifting on the fly as they react to your words. Sometimes we do this as a practical matter — we're selling a product, an idea, ourselves — but most often we do it for no other reason than trying to control our image.

There are two problems with trying to control our image. First, it's impossible. We can never dictate what people will think of us, and frequently, the harder we try, the more convinced they become of their initial perceptions. Second, placing such importance on what people think of us leads to a constant wariness, a vigilance that locks us right up.

The good news is that our need in this regard is a foolproof sign. Whatever irks us about our image, in anyone's eyes, points directly to a part of ourselves that we're seriously resisting. Wherever we still care, resistance is there.

I hate it, for example, when people think I talk too much. Why? Because sometimes I *do* talk too much. I wish it were different, wish I had made more progress with this embarrassing habit. The truth, however, is that there are still many times when it gets the best of me.

All of us would like to be seen in certain ways. Nothing wrong with that — it's just a preference. But often that preference can harden into expectation. How to tell the difference? Just follow the resistance.

Expectation, for everyone, is another resistance machine. It yanks us from the present with an abstraction, a need, a certainty that can never be trusted. Acceptance, on the other hand, permits us to pursue preferences without closing down. And sometimes, without pursuing anything at all, we still uncover hidden treasures.

CHAPTER 28

Hidden Treasures

When the barriers of our personality become
porous, we encounter life more directly.

WHETHER SHATTERED BY accident or design, if we remain open the experience enthralls us. We find that our field of awareness just grows and grows. All the things we assumed we were now flow along in an ever-shifting array. Thoughts, feelings, desires, sensations — they encompass the experience of life without defining us. Wiring, biography, perspective, preference — they steer our course but aren't the ship itself. So then where is this ship, we wonder. What is it made of? Just who, we come to ask, am I?

Who am I? At first glance such a question can seem rhetorical, adolescent, or irrelevant to everyday life. But if we're no longer identifying with the phenomena of experience, if we're no longer clinging to or resisting what arises, then answering this question takes on vital importance. Without an answer we can easily become disoriented, aimless.

Many religions and philosophies have a ready-made response, but adopting one on faith risks the same type of contraction as a fiercely held opinion. It is best, as always, to reach our own findings from our own experience. Yet it is also a mistake to assume that there's a fixed or final answer. Instead, relying on our new practice, we can choose to live the question.

Living this particular question — *Who am I?* — never fails to bring up a host of related concerns. We begin to wrestle with the purpose of life, with its meaning. Among the most common conclusions: We are here to grow; to learn; to heal; to serve others; to serve God; to have fun; to love.

While conclusions like these are deeply personal, they're also just ideas. They provide a story, an interpretation for something beyond the power of thought to grasp. They satisfy, from time to time, a restless, swinging mind. But to show up in the moment completely, to do these new questions justice, requires that we let them be.

Sometimes, without any answers to hold onto, it seems like we're nothing at all. Other times, overwhelmed by life's roaring torrent, it seems like we're everything at once. These two impressions are actually flipsides of the same coin. They're a taste of what happens when the barriers of our personality become porous. We encounter life directly, without anything to mediate its intensity. We see clearly, in those moments, how the self we carry with us is no more or less than a tool of our organism, a system that allows us to function, but that also, miraculously, we have the ability to step right through.

Whenever this stepping through occurs, be it for one moment or a million, we find ourselves subsumed by great and indescribable forces, as seductive as they are untamable. These hidden treasures are ours to have, but not to hold. First among them, of course, is bliss. A joyous, loving heart radiates naturally from this *trans*personal space.

But bliss isn't the only gift on this journey. Often we gain a sense of life's deepest rhythms. This is known in Hinduism as Shakti, in Hebrew as Ruach, in Christianity as the Holy Spirit, and in pop culture as The Zone. None of these terms means exactly the same thing, but they each describe aspects of what can grace us from the regions beyond the "I."

In Jungian psychology, this reservoir outside the self is referred to as the Self. This terminology suggests that each of us possesses a dual identity. Seen from one vantage point we're a specific "I," but from another we're eternally united with all that is. We will explore the concept of dual identity a little later, but for now let's keep our focus trained on individual experience.

For many, "peak" experiences are what lead to a direct encounter with the Self. For some it comes through spiritual practices like meditation or yoga. For others it's always with them, like a subtle wind in life's background. Still others touch this landscape periodically, through paranormal manifestations such as intuition, ESP, or out of body episodes.

The self and the Self can seem mutually exclusive, like distant lands across a wide gulf. But what bridges that gulf is the part of us that witnesses everything, the part that watches life's parade like a steady, impassive camera. This Witness, which exists in everyone, calmly observes the surroundings in both lands. The Witness notices, moment by moment, that we can shift instantly between one and the other. It also records the way that both can exist at once. Because personal experience is what we're most familiar with, transpersonal experience often seems quite fantastic. In some cultures, however, the two states enjoy equal footing. There, to touch the Self can be a daily, hourly, or sometimes almost constant occurrence.

The greatest gateway to the Self is acceptance, presence, a consistent and skillful non-doing. In other words, living the questions is our free ticket. But passage comes with a definite trade-off. We must be willing to surrender our sense of personal control and let the Self determine life's flow. We must accept that flow when it's rough-and-tumble, even unbearable, and not just when the going's good. We must expand wider than ever before, nearing total dissolution, to make room for the most exquisite mystery.

CHAPTER 29

Mystery

*The only way to achieve maximum openness is to
arrive at every single moment without preconception.*

AS WE EXPLORE THE TRANS-
personal terrain, as we dance with dissolution, the "I" often screams
bloody murder. It senses a coup, the end of its domain, and will
do just about anything to protect that turf. Waiting in its arsenal,
on hand for this climactic battle, are the most tenacious types of
contraction.

FIREWORKS

Usually, of the three we'll discuss, the first weapon launched
is the "new convert" contraction. A taste of the Self, with its waves
of power and delight, can cause us to become fixated on the fire-
works and to turn our backs on the everyday. We decide that
we've "found it," and begin summoning the Self at every opportunity. Whether we get there through God or a guru, on our own
or in community, all we want is that spiritual high.

But if there's a high, then there must be a low. Clinging to the
Self is like any other clinging. It causes us to contract against

whatever else comes, especially when it's about such "mundane" matters as doing the laundry or paying the bills. It also causes us to condescend toward people who haven't discovered the same path. Surprisingly, resistance occurs just as often outside the self as it does within. And when it does, as always, we find ourselves flung from the moment.

PUFFING UP

A second common contraction is mistaking the lower case for the upper, believing that self and Self are one and the same. In this instance we survey the transpersonal landscape like real estate, and seek to annex it as part of a mightier "I." We feel special to have made it this far, to be chosen, and puff up with the supposed distinction. Instead of surrendering control we attempt to re-assert it, to turn the flow of life in a self-serving direction.

This happens on a grand scale with corrupt preachers and masters, who betray their flocks in the name of higher powers. Often, since the possession of these powers is precisely what elicits such trust and support, the betrayals are a double tragedy.

The same thing happens on a lesser scale with many types of "energetic" healers. They pretend to own what comes through them, or to codify its inherent mystery. That's not to say that the elements of healing can't be taught or explained, just that their practice requires the ultimate humility. Without it, too easily, personal agendas can pose as God's will.

This can also happen to ordinary people, to any one of us,

when we stop showing up completely for every moment. Not showing up, in this context, means believing that our understanding is now complete. With the arrival of new and profound experience, with glimpses of deeper wisdom, we begin to assume that life will invariably conform to what we've learned. Worse yet, we become supposed translators of life's agenda, proclaiming what is and isn't in universal harmony.

A deep connection to the environment, for example, might lead us to help protect the rainforest. We might devote time, money, and skill toward the preservation of a specific region, all of which stems from our preference that it doesn't disappear. No problem so far, just a willingness to pursue our goal. But the minute we decide that our goal *must* be achieved, that the fate of Mother Nature hangs in the balance, we've crossed the line into serious contraction.

Truth is, we simply can't know the ultimate purpose of anything. Perhaps, in this instance, destruction of the region is what finally galvanizes the public. A temporary setback, just maybe, is what enables an eventual victory.

Yet beyond the duality of winning and losing, such destruction might possess no purpose whatsoever. It may merely be what is. No matter how much our perspective encompasses the transpersonal, it's still just a limited view. The whys and wherefores of any event are never something we can totally fathom. Some chalk this up to karma, or a divine plan, but even those conceptions can feed our need for an orderly universe.

Showing up in the face of what affronts us, of what violates our sense of the sacred, means accepting things that make no sense. For every synchronistic occurrence that suggests all things happen for a reason, there may be an equal explosion of chaos that signals the exact opposite. Living the questions fully, with real courage, requires embracing that contradiction.

PRETENDING TO KNOW

Closer to home, full of a newfound reverence for life, we often advise our loved ones from a presumption of greater knowing. This happened to me when a friend of mine fell prey to serious addiction. I counseled him constantly that such self-destruction wasn't in his best interest. The more he spun out of control, the more I contracted against him. How could such harmful behavior need to be a part of what is? I was certain it didn't, until my friend hit complete bottom.

There, with nothing left to hang onto, he finally allowed himself to shatter and heal. The depth of his transformation was astounding. I had to admit, in retrospect, that it couldn't have occurred as fully had he taken my earlier advice.

But even if things hadn't ended happily, even if he had overdosed and died, I wouldn't have been a bit more right. Only my full acceptance of his choices, even to the point of death, would have kept me totally present. Out of love and compassion we can always speak up, but living the questions calls us to temper all guidance with uncertainty and to stay open when it isn't heeded.

Often, staying open presents the greatest challenge when it's our own lives that seem mysteriously thwarted. We live the questions, tap the source, and revel in bliss without our circumstances improving. We know there's no direct correlation, that the bliss of being is unrelated to external conditions. Still, we can't escape the sneaking suspicion that we're doing something wrong. We wonder why we're not getting more healthy, or finding the perfect partner, or breaking through blocks at work.

In my film career, whenever I've encountered a periodic dry spell, it's been tempting to contract against the situation and over-think every move. Should I alter my style? Change agents? Write in a different genre? But on close inspection, such analysis often reveals false pride. Much as the "I" doesn't get it, no amount of spiritual conviction ever bestows omniscience. Strategy can help streamline our efforts, but it can never guarantee results. Whether I push harder or give up, change tactics or steady the course, the ending of a dry spell will forever remain as mysterious as its onset.

THE FALLACY OF SELF-IMPROVEMENT

The third and final contraction that besets us at this juncture is also the thorniest. It arises out of a genuine will toward personal growth. Without any undue inflation, we may study the transpersonal like eager students. We may learn new types of spiritual practice, or martial arts, or attend cutting-edge weekends and workshops. We may devour the sacred texts, push ourselves to the limit, and undertake great austerities.

In and of themselves, none of these activities presents a problem. But slowly, if we neglect to live the questions, the fallacy of
self-improvement seeps in. We begin to fall in love with the "I,"
with our collection of new attributes, and in the process shore up
all that's been shattered. This striving for perfection keeps the
Self at bay, erects barricades against the fullness of the moment.
As well-meaning as our efforts may be, the "I" co-opts them for
less laudable purposes.

The only way to achieve maximum openness is to arrive at
every moment without a single preconception. Otherwise, we
resist what doesn't fit our model. Regardless of how much we
know, or how evolved we've become, we must put every bit of
that aside. We must step into the mystery naked and undefended.
We must practice what Zen refers to as "beginner's mind."

Beginner's mind is akin to the wisdom of Socrates, who said
"All I know is that I know nothing." This kind of humble awareness leads to great receptivity. It allows for maximum discovery.
It ensures that our new and improved lenses don't just become
blinders. Complexity, if we let it, is what enables us to stay strik-
ingly simple.

Along with beginner's mind comes a freedom as delectable as
bliss. We're even willing to set bliss aside, if choosing it doesn't
serve the moment. Living the questions with such radical expansion never ceases to suffuse us with wonder. Be it minuscule or
massive, glorious or horrific, every aspect of creation glows. Instead of just acknowledging, or observing, we're willing to expe-

rience the mystery firsthand. And then, eventually, we embody the mystery ourselves.

CHAPTER 30

More Mystery

We experience our existence, simultaneously,
in both the relative and the absolute.

WHEN I WAS IN SECOND grade, my best friend had a stock response to insults. He'd screw up his face in anger and yell, "I'm rubber, you're glue. Whatever you say bounces off me and sticks to you."

A few years later, in Sunday school, a rabbi lectured my class about criticism. "We often find the faults in others," he told us, "that we are least able to see in ourselves."

Recently, I realized that my friend and the rabbi were saying the same thing. Projection, it turns out, isn't just the province of ethics or psychology. It's an idea so elementary that it permeates the playground. As discussed earlier, projection occurs when we mistake the inside for the outside. Introjection occurs when we mistake the outside for the inside. Clearly, each is a mirror of the other. Why they happen at all, however, can seem anything but clear.

The past two chapters have explored the way that living the questions, over time, breaks down the boundaries between self and Self. We come to see that the division between ourselves and the rest of the world is an illusion. It's an illusion which allows us to function, but one we eventually learn to see through. Seeing through the illusion of separateness is what solves the riddle of the inside and the outside.

The answer to the riddle is that neither inside nor outside exist. In fact, they are one and the same. On a fundamental level, we are the world. Likewise, the world is us. No wonder, then, that I'm rubber and you're glue. No wonder that the faults I find in you might also be my own.

This principle is observable in every aspect of life. Science, for example, demonstrates that interdependence between the elements of nature is what enables life to exist. From the air we breathe to the food we eat to the love we share, none of us is ever an island. We all function, or malfunction, as a whole.

The visceral sensation of this unity is what many encounter when they taste the transpersonal. It's what the mystics celebrate in all their texts (see chapter 16). But it can also be explored and experienced in any of our lives, in any moment. Working with emotions is a great place to start.

FLASHPOINTS

Take the way we respond to flaws in our friends. Some of them seem harmless, delightful even. At the same time, other flaws cause us to contract with rage. So what's the difference? Why the flare-up? From my experience, there is a formula at work. The more emotion such a flaw arouses, the deeper it reflects something inside us.

This may sound like a restatement of the rabbi's adage, yet it isn't. Often, the flaw in a friend doesn't mirror a similar flaw in ourselves, but rather *a part of us that we've contracted against.*

I have a thing, for example, about friends who don't return phone calls. Un-returned calls are something I truly can't stand. Consequently, I return every one of my own calls with almost compulsive speed. I strive to be respectful, responsible, and contract against the opposite wherever it occurs. And that's just the point. I'm so aligned with responsibility that any impulses to let things slide, or to blow someone off, are resisted bitterly in my inner world.

But they're there, nevertheless, and the flashpoint of each new unreturned call is proof positive. As soon as I accept these impulses in myself, fully, the experience will no longer carry such a charge. I'll just call again to check in, or wait patiently, like I do when someone's late for an appointment. No flashpoint there, since a slight bent toward tardiness is something for which I've long ago forgiven myself.

Let me state the formula another way. The deeper something is repressed within us, the more forcefully it will appear outside us. Consciousness, in this way, is like a Möbius strip — one seamless, unified experience that appears divided in two. Whenever we find ourselves triggered, having a huge emotional reaction, it's a reminder of this inherent fusion.

A sculptor I know detected this in his troubled marriage. It's his dream to make a full-time living at his craft, but so far he's had to fall back on teaching at the local high school. His wife doesn't really support his dream, mostly because she questions his talent. Rarely is this expressed overtly — it's too painful for both of them — but every once in awhile it slips out.

During a recent argument, it did slip out. But with tempers flaring, the sculptor gained enough awareness to live the questions. Right then, in the heat of the moment, here's what he found:

What is happening right now?

> I'm angry. And frustrated. Why won't she believe in me?! How can I be married to someone like that?!

Can I be with it?

> Why should I?! I deserve so much better!

What is happening right now?

> The more I try to make her understand, the less she does. She keeps contracting against me. I keep contracting against her.

At this point, the sculptor hit on a key discovery. An argument always occurs within us at the same time it's happening without. Even more than attacking his wife, he was trying to *stop feeling his own pain*. In an act of dire futility, he was both lashing out and saying "make me better."

Remember our "stepping on the hose" analogy? Here's another perfect example. But in this case it was even worse, since now there were *two* hoses equally squashed.

Realizing this, asking for a time-out, the sculptor continued to live the questions.

What is happening right now?

> I'm contracted, resisting. There's something I don't want to feel. It must be about her not believing in me. Just the thought of that drives me crazy.

Can I be with it?

> With the feeling of not being believed in? Oh, boy. That's a tough one. Goes way back.

What is happening right now?

> I'm realizing there's a part of me that doesn't believe in myself. Locked away, but strong. No wonder we keep having this fight. Every time she doubts me, it's like salt on the wound.

By staying present, the sculptor learned how the shortcoming he saw in his wife was a reflection of his own very deep contraction. The issue between them didn't go away, but from then on they handled it differently. They could talk about it without exploding. And each of them, separately, began to explore their feelings about success, failure, creativity, and repression. In the process, they "took back" the projections they had shone on one another. They grew to accept the Möbius strip of their marriage.

One final, more pleasant reminder of the Möbius strip is the way two open hearts connect. When we want to feel love for another person, we bring attention to our own heart. We go in, as it were, to go out. Conversely, many people can't access love internally. They need to *be* loved in order to feel love. This, of course, is going out to get in. Either way, in the moment, the love that arises can't tell the difference. It stops time, bridges distance, melts us with indivisible union.

A DOUBLE DESTINY

An entire school of Hindu thought is devoted to this unifying approach. It's called Advaita, which simply means "not two." Advaita claims that each moment unfolds in utter perfection, with utter wholeness, and that nothing could be other than it is. Whether we contract or expand, change or stagnate, it's all a foregone conclusion.

Our worst mistake, according to Advaita, is believing in the self at all. It's a kind of reverse atheism, maintaining that you and I are the illusion, and that only God exists. A direct experience of this self-erasure, of the mystic's Holy Grail, can provide an astounding liberation. It's a flash of essence, which can hasten our shattering or profoundly renew it. But it can also wreak havoc with our day-to-day lives. Drowning in Oneness, after all, is still drowning.

If everything is perfect, then what difference does it make
what I do? If everything is God, then why does being me matter
even one bit? Questions like these arise inevitably when we drown
in Oneness. They paralyze us with indecision, strip away our
sense of direction. Ironically, too much expansion leads to a new
type of contraction. We begin to cling to the universal and deny
the particular. In other words, we stop seeing the trees for the
forest.

Living the questions in the light of Oneness requires rare skill.
It demands that we embrace the ultimate paradox, that we see
the forest *and* the trees, the self *and* the Self. The blessings of
existence show up just as often in seeming separateness as they
do in Oneness. Snow, basketball, orgasm, pizza — each of us has
our own list of distinct miracles. And life's endless stream of lesser
stuff — pencils, taxes, snoring, shoes — in a different way is
equally amazing.

Living the questions in the light of Oneness calls us to a double
destiny. We experience our existence, simultaneously, in both the
relative and the absolute. We learn to grasp the fabric but be the
thread. This allows us to make choices, take sides, and pursue our
passions like everyone else. It makes it possible for us to develop
and exult in our own uniqueness. All the while, however, we stay
connected to the greater glory. As a result, we don't usually take
ourselves too seriously. We spot resistance early and release it
with ease. We cherish the mystery within every moment, as infinite as it is specific.

Living the questions in the light of Oneness is a melding of assertion and surrender, motion and stillness, curiosity and conviction. We accept everything, yet stop at nothing.

CHAPTER 31

Greater Mystery Still

THE IDEA FOR THIS BOOK CAME to me during my daily meditation. It grew stronger over a few week's time. Soon I found myself taking notes, and then whole passages began to flow. It wasn't always easy or smooth, however. Living the questions, I noticed that one part of me was reticent, bashful, daunted by the fact that everything has already been said. At the same time, a conflicting part of me just wanted to sing out, to add another voice to the choir.

It's true that there's nothing new under the sun, yet it's equally true that you can't step into the same river twice. So I came to heed my own words, to honor the universal without denying the personal. As a result I felt the choir inside, supporting me, harmonizing as I sung my solo.

Throughout the writing process, I fantasized about what would happen when the book was finished. I saw myself at store signings, in magazines, and on *Oprah*. This is akin to the way every screenwriter dreams up an Oscar speech before finishing the first draft. I'm used to it by now. It's always good for a laugh. But it doesn't keep me from living the questions, from acknowledging that the fate of the completed work is largely out of my hands. Talk shows are possible, but so is the prospect of no publication whatsoever. Perhaps the result of all this bliss will remain in a trunk, long forgotten, to be discovered decades from now by an inquisitive relative.

Whatever occurs, whether these words reach just one or a multitude, I want to express my gratitude that you took the journey. As I wrote in the beginning, I hope that it doesn't end here. I hope you test every one of my observations in the laboratory of your own life and that you let personal experience yield the final verdict.

Relish what works, toss what doesn't, and pass on whatever you can. All the while keep your eyes wide open. Invariably, choosing to live the questions leads to virgin territory. Without the aid of a roadmap, you'll cherish what fellow pilgrims you find.

Soon, as your time with this book fades into memory, most of its points will fade away, too. No problem there — that's just how it works. But to live the questions well, in any situation, all you need to remember are a few key concepts...

Contraction — *an instinctive response to anything unwanted*

Expansion — *the state of connectedness to all things*

Resistance — *the choice, conscious or otherwise, to remain contracted*

Awareness — *enough separation from resistance to recognize it's there*

Acceptance — *the allowing and embracing of all experience*

Presence — *the moment to moment process of acceptance*

Bliss — *joy plus love minus cause, the song of the heart, ever-expanding*

Then, of course, there are the questions themselves.

What is happening right now?

Can I be with it?

Living those questions is saying yes to life, to all of it, and especially to its radiant mystery. That mystery is what brought us both to this moment, and will stay with us for the rest of our days. Because no matter how well we live the questions right now, we never know what happens next.

Gratitude

THIS BOOK WAS NURTURED into being by the loving spirit of many. I want to express my gratitude, first of all, to Stephany Evans, super agent and desert sage, whose commitment to the project was, and still is, inspiring. A heartfelt thank you to my insightful group of early readers, who patiently helped tease the manuscript into its final detail and clarity. They are: Mary Beth Albert, Josh Baran, Elise Cannon, Lynda Harvey, Leslie Jonath, Terry Patten, and Kate Taylor. I'd also like to thank the whole team at Quest for sharing and shaping the book's vision.

Enduring gratitude to my family, Frieda, Randi, Bruce, Andrew, Emmy, Sharon, Jake, Eli, Frederic, Margie, Felton and Boone. A special note of thanks to Robert Cushnir, my father, who has supported all my ventures even at their most mystifying.

Our truest friends and supporters simply bear witness for us through lilfe's challenges. If they point out our resistance from time to time, and nudge us greatly toward acceptance, then the treasure is that much greater. In this regard my above-mentioned readers have all served double duty, and have been joined along the way by Ann Armstrong, Cynthia Bissonnette, Cynthia Hagen, Marilyn Hershenson, Barbara Molle, Tom Paris, Lorraine Soderberg,

Mercedes Terezza, Frederic Wiedemann, and Adam Wolff.

In addition, I am indebted to the brave, authentic souls who have allowed me to reproduce their inner dialogues within these pages.

Finally, my deepest gratitude to all those who have lived the questions throughout the ages and left us a record of their journey. Mystics, pilgrims, rebels, saints — their voices have given rise to my own and have bridged the way to bliss.

QUEST BOOKS
are published by
The Theosophical Society in America,
Wheaton, Illinois 60189-0270,
a branch of a world fellowship,
a membership organization
dedicated to the promotion of the unity of
humanity and the encouragement of the study of
religion, philosophy, and science, to the end that
we may better understand ourselves and our place in
the universe. The Society stands for complete
freedom of individual search and belief.
For further information about its activities,
write, call 1-800-669-1571, e-mail olcott@theosophia.org,
or consult its Web page: http://www.theosophical.org

The Theosophical Publishing House
is aided by the generous support of
THE KERN FOUNDATION,
a trust established by Herbert A. Kern
and dedicated to Theosophical education.

UNCONDITIONAL BLISS
Finding Happiness in the Face of Hardship

◆ ◆ ◆

Unconditional Bliss *is a wonderful distillation of the classical spiritual approach to life: bringing awareness and a transformed relationship to whatever we are presented with. It is practical, refreshing, and a lot of fun to read.*

—Sharon Salzberg, author of *Lovingkindness* and
A Heart as Wide as the World

This indispensable handbook for spiritual well-being will satisfy even the harshest skeptics. Simple, direct, and deeply joyful, Cushnir's wonderful volume will help everyone struggling for happiness—the sort that lasts—in our complex and challenging world.

—Mark Matousek, author of *Sex Death Enlightenment*
and *Dialogues with a Modern Mystic*

Unconditional Bliss *brings a fresh, insightful, important approach to the fullness of the present moment. It makes clear that all other growth and spiritual enrichment must begin with attention to what is happening right now. The book is written in a tone both clear and practical, honest and wise. It will appeal to readers of all persuasions. Howard Cushnir can help us plumb life's mystery and joy.*

—Lama Surya Das, author of *Awakening the Buddha
Within* and *Awakening to the Sacred*